Dedicated to all those wonderful dogs who deserve more in their lives; better care, greater respect, and increased kindness with a broader understanding of their needs as sentient, social, and loving creatures.

Table of Contents

All thanks and gratitude to all the dogs and their families that

I have been privileged to work with over the years - without

whom no word of this book could have been written.

***

TO PROTECT THE PRIVACY OF THE DOGS AND THEIR

FAMILIES NAMES AND PICTURES MAY HAVE BEEN CHANGED

***

All Thanks to Snuffy

In the words of a very wise Madame Germaine de Staël
"The more I see of man, the more I like dogs."

This resonates with me, and so many of us, because of the truth in the statement. The only error may be in the word "like" because I love my dogs. More than that even - I adore them, I respect them, I appreciate them. I have always felt a connection with dogs and, in turn always had a certain magic with them. A magic that I took for granted until I started working with dogs everyday as a boarding kennel owner and animal rescue foster home. That is when I realized that my "way with dogs" was indeed special and not something that every person is lucky enough to be gifted with.

My life has been tied to dogs since my childhood in very significant ways. My first dog was a Poodle that my mom bought at the local pet store when I was seven years old. Snuffy was an adorable, grey Toy Poodle - so tiny, so fluffy, and so sick. Snuffy had parvovirus. All his siblings from the litter ended up succumbing to the devastating illness but Snuffy survived. I remember having to feed him with an eyedropper but, of course, my mom provided most of the round the clock care he required which ultimately saved his life. I guess there are real, tangible benefits to a puppy having a nurse take him home! Snuffy was a survivor - we saved his life. Little did we know that just weeks later he would return the favor.

It was just days before Christmas. Outside it was cold and snowy, of course, given we lived in the middle of Canada. My family was warm and cozy inside though, fast asleep in our beds for the night. I had for whatever "baby of the family" reason, invited myself to sleep in my mom's bed that night. As such, she was relegated to just a few inches of mattress on her side of the queen bed (I was a bit of a kicker I am told). Perhaps that is why her arm was dangling off the side of the bed. My mom was roused from her slumber by our puppy whining and licking her hand that hung down and out from under the covers. She grumbled for Snuffy to let

her sleep but then in an instant, she was awake - she smelled

smoke! She tried to wake me without much success so she

ran down the hall to my sister's room, screaming for my

seventeen-year-old brother to get up, as smoke accumulated

at a frightening rate. It took great effort because of the

effects of the smoke, but she was eventually able to wake my

Copy of newspaper clipping detailing the fire and how Snuffy saved our lives

older sister. With my siblings up, we all gathered in my mom's bedroom, which was not only as far from the fire as possible, but also afforded a means of escape - out the window and onto the roof of our garage. With the door closed and soaked towels placed where possible to prevent smoke seeping in, mom's comforter was tossed out the window and we all in turn climbed out. It was not easy given the style of window, but my brother was there to help navigate us through if we got stuck.

Once we were all out, including Snuffy of course, my brother went for help. He was a superhero that night - despite the height and the nearly foot deep snow, he jumped down to the ground via a car roof and hood, and ran to our neighbors. He was stuck having to yell and almost break down their door to help us. It was the middle of the night and they were terrified that someone was trying to violently break in. *No! Just pick up your phone and call the Fire Department now please!!!* He returned with a ladder and helped us all down and into our neighbor's house - with Snuffy in tow.

While I owe a lot to my family for getting me through that night, my family really owes our lives to Snuffy. The little puppy that made it up the stairs for the very first time that night to wake up my mom and save us all. When I was older, I was the only one of my siblings living with my mom and stepfather. I was fortunate enough to be allowed to get a dog, Max, from our local SPCA. We tried to say she was my Mother's Day gift for my mom but she ended up being my birthday present instead. Max was a gorgeous Black Lab, Springer Spaniel cross that a family had surrendered to the SPCA because she got so big. She was an incredible dog and my heart still swells when I think of her now. I do not think I truly enjoyed anything more in my life at that time than when Max and I would go exploring for hours in and around the property we rented. We lived in an agricultural area, so we could hike for hours to find new paths, spot wildlife, or just sit together contemplating life while admiring a gorgeous view. Those times were so wonderful because I was satisfying my curiosity and sense of adventure for exploring new   places, feeling confident and strong in spite of my insecurities and sharing them with a companion with whom I had a

A young me with a young Max

loving and trusting connection during a period when I was struggling to feel loved by anyone. Even in the darkest of times for me, spending time with Max was always a blessing. She could heal my heart and soul. She was there whenever I needed her, to listen, to love, and to be loved. She was the dog that truly taught me the truth of the adage "a dog is a man's best friend."

It was decades later that we took on operating a boarding kennel. I had never worked in a kennel before but had confidence in my business acumen coupled with faith in my innate ability to connect with dogs. Within a few weeks of operating our business, I was fostering dogs for our local

Humane Society. My husband, Jeff, and I had our own family - 2 sons, 3 dogs, and too many cats, but I felt strongly that we should help animals in need whenever and however we could. In our years running the kennel, we were blessed to not only work with hundreds of client's furry family members but also with hundreds of rescued dogs looking for their happily forever after. The Humane Society had a large network of private foster homes but we were able to provide care for those more challenging dogs, along with providing care for greater numbers of dogs when groups needed to come into care.

I not only assessed the dogs, but would also work to rehabilitate the more challenging dogs in order to greatly improve their chances at successful adoption. Whether it was fear, aggression, detachment, or any other undesirable behavior, I would develop a plan and work through the rehabilitation with that dog to help them overcome their issues. The goal of the rehabilitation was always to find the dog on the other side of any issues, to achieve a balanced confidence in themselves, to discover who the dog truly was so we could find the best forever home specifically for them. Rehabilitating to that level requires a lot of time, patience, and insight along with specific environmental and social needs that not all rescues can provide. That is what made the work I did so special. Working every single day with dogs of all sizes, breeds, and behaviors was exhausting, demanding, and often stressful, but even more so – it was a true gift. The Humane Society was committed to not simply adopting a dog out as quickly as possible to the first person or family to apply but to finding the best forever family for that dog. Given the Executive Director's vast experience working in rescue and rehoming thousands of dogs, she supported my work with the dogs since she knew all too often the dog's true personality could hide behind its problems and without rehabilitation, our adoption successes would be limited.

All too often rescues simply adopt a dog out without being able to work through such issues. The best-case scenario is the adopters finding the dog's personality to not be what they had wanted once they can overcome the problem behaviors. The worst-case scenario is when dogs lose their lives due to reactivity or aggression because the adopters – and the rescue – were ill equipped to help them. Some rescues will say they cannot address aggression issues due to liability reasons, offloading these dogs to the best-intentioned adopters and simply advising them to seek out a trainer. However, we believed it was far better - even in regards to liability - to help dogs as soon as possible given the resources and experience we had available. I could provide care specifically designed for the needs of the dog throughout its rehabilitation that most households simply could not. It was not easy but it was beyond worth it when I would find the perfect family for that dog - a dog that had blossomed into who they were meant to be because of the care I provided.

It was the most rewarding work I have ever done and provided me with insights into the ways of dogs. I chose to operate our kennel how I felt was healthiest for the dogs. The dogs would exercise and socialize in groups at least four times a day - off-leash on the secure property. I initially would leash walk the dogs on the rural roads or the paths in the forested park neighboring our property – but this proved to be too unpredictable to be safe for the dogs in our care. I needed to not only assure our dog clients were not injured but also found that the dog's freedom to exercise and socialize as they were comfortable was of the greatest benefit to their wellbeing. When not outside and supervised, they enjoyed being safe and comfortable inside in their own spaces to eat, drink, and sleep. I wanted to really facilitate dogs being allowed to just be dogs. It seemed to be what made the dogs relaxed, happy, and confident. In managing the dogs this way, I witnessed how dogs choose to live, behave, and interact when left to be dogs. The motivation was to provide dogs a standard of care that would be best for them but the invaluable result was a window into their world. No owners around, no micromanaging of their behavior, and no unreasonable expectations of them. The dogs were simply provided a safe environment to be themselves, to exercise and socialize, to play and explore, to just enjoy their life however they chose to, in that moment, on that day.

I quickly realized that dogs were able to teach, motivate, and support each other in ways that we, as humans, could not. The dogs I had could help me teach other dogs the ways of the world. Their help in rehabilitating dogs was invaluable and significant in a number of ways if I carefully selected which dogs and at what time in the process. This recognition of the dogs as teachers and role models themselves allowed

Quality time with my teachers

me to fully embrace and respect that dogs have more to give than we typically allow.

The dogs taught me things that are even more important when I realized how their interactions and choices were applicable and relevant to people and society. This book is a collection of these insights that I share in hopes that others will benefit from the same invaluable lessons that dogs taught me. These lessons that only a true best friend could share and that in times of doubt or reflection make me now ask "What would Dogs do?"

The Best of FUR-iends

In our lives we will encounter all sorts of lessons to learn - some are easy and straightforward, and others are more challenging to hear let alone understand and learn from. There are things about ourselves that actually create the negative experiences we have; we have a tendency to be in denial of our own faults, or perhaps we simply cannot recognize them as abnormal given how and where we were raised or have lived. We go out into the world and make mistakes. We get into trouble. There is a tendency to want to deflect

One of my best friends, Teddy

blame onto circumstance or onto others - when in truth we typically have a role to play in what has occurred. It is in these times of personal struggle and reflection that our fair-weather friends leave or betray us, good friends stand by us and listen to us - but best friends have the unconditional love for us that allows them to tell us truths that others would never dare.

Best friends will share those hurtful truths because in the end they only want what is best for us; to overcome, to heal, to grow in order to avoid similar struggles recurring. Their love for us sees through the facades of ego, doubt, pride, and self-pity to who we are, who we can be, and who we should be. They believe in our potential being so much greater than we even recognize. They lay out the hard truth and then stand by us as we work through our challenges or pain to gain strength from those lessons and move on to being our best selves. Their goal is to see us living our best lives in hopes that we will be that best friend they need when they stumble in their lives.

Best friends are not best friends because it is easy - best friends are best friends because of love. Love is not easy but love is powerful. Love is the motivation. Love is the answer to why they dig deep and support us with steadfast resolve. Love is why the best of friends are with us as we weather whatever storm we may be facing. This kind of unconditional love is the love a dog has for his human. Our dogs love us in real and tangible ways.

Dogs seek out connection with us and are present both physically and emotionally. They are always happy to see us

Initially fearful Sleddies making a connection through a kiss

without any concern for how we look, who we love, or what we believe. They play with us when we are happy, snuggle us when we are sad, and stand by us when we are scared. The relationship is authentic. All you have to do is look into your dog's eyes to see the connection that is formed from which affection and love were born. The bond between owner and dog is unique and extremely valuable to both parties.

Our dogs are so important in our lives as companions and confidantes, they simply cannot be replaced by another. It is why the adage that a dog is a man's best friend has endured and resonated for centuries. Some may say that dogs are our best friend because they were always there for us. Others that they were always there for us because a best friend always is. I think both are true. Even if it is a friendship that began out of simply sharing space, it has proven to be treasured by man and dog alike. We always refer to dogs as our best friends because they were, are, and will be throughout our existence.

In my early twenties, I commuted downtown for work every day. One day like the next, very routine, and unremarkable. All except one day, I vividly remember a very angry homeless man on my way to work. As anyone who lives in a major center will know, someone on the street asking for money, relying on the kindness of strangers, will usually attempt to be at least cordial. However, this man was beyond niceties with the strangers walking by him. He was hurt and frustrated. He was standing there on a corner, lunging at all those walking by, screaming "I am a human being! I am a human! You treat your dogs better than you treat me!" It was both unnerving and heartbreaking. He was so aggressive and distraught - but even more than that - he was right. Over the past several decades, there has been a shift in the way people think about and care for their dogs. Dogs have transitioned from the outdoors to in. Dogs are invited into our homes, onto our couches, and beside us in bed at night. Dogs have truly become members of our families - like never before in our shared evolutionary history. Occasionally dogs are even "replacements" for family members! How many times have you heard someone say their dogs are their children? Dog owners often anthropomorphize their beloved hounds and treat them as if they are human. Not only buying them human grade food, but memory foam beds, enrichment toys, and costumes for Halloween.

As heartwarming as it is to share our lives with our dogs, people who have enmeshed their dogs into their lives have been challenged to teach the dogs how to live a human lifestyle. Our mutually beneficial relationship is a centuries old friendship between Homo sapiens and Canines but the dynamics of that relationship have shifted. People love their dogs an incredible amount, but in treating them as if they are human, we have lost respect for dogs as dogs. As a result, dog owners can struggle with their dogs' behavior and training because we expect them to act like humans. This expectation is unfair and completely unreasonable. Thousands of books have been written, television shows produced, millions of dollars spent on trainers, millions of online searches and video views, and even movies produced to help people understand and train their dogs. Occasionally, people will even get dogs seemingly to just serve as a fashion or lifestyle accessory and are overwhelmed with how to deal with the dog as a sentient, living, breathing, shedding, barking, urinating, defecating, exercise-needing being. We love dogs so much, have so much to share with them, and so much we want to teach them. All this to give but we definitely seem to demand a return. In exchange for what we give, we often place pressure and expectation on them to behave in ways that may be natural to us, but certainly are not at all, natural to dogs. Dogs do not always act predictably or desirably in our world and homes.

It is easy to forget they are dogs, to see them as human as we share our homes, lives, and hearts with them. Given the connection I have with dogs, I have a unique ability to relate to them and somehow understand how they are feeling and what they are thinking. In living with many dogs throughout my life and working with hundreds over the past several years, I always saw correlations in the behavior of human beings and dogs. I did not realize the depth nor the breadth of these correlations until working with dogs as my career - my immersion into dogdom. A key to validating my observations as true was the apparent relevance of Maslow's Hierarchy of Needs to dogs, their motivations, and the needs in their existence. By working with such a multitude of dogs – especially those in need of rehabilitation for behavioral challenges – the applicability became obvious.

I learned of Maslow's work years ago in university in one of my psychology classes. It resonated as true to me at the time and I carried that knowledge into my understanding of both consumer and human behavior in my career. He asserted that one has to achieve certain levels of existence before being able to do more or be more. His hierarchy levels are (in ranking order) Physiological, Safety, Love/Belonging, Esteem, and finally Self-Actualization. Physiological needs – air, food, water, shelter, etc. – are the highest priority for humans and are necessary before one worries about safety.

You can see this in actions of those that will risk their personal safety to acquire those physiological needs: severe thirst leading to drinking dirty water, risk punishment for theft but so hungry will steal food, surface to breathe even if trying to hide under water. Safety is important but always secondary to basic life support needs of air, water, and food. The third level is love, as in relationships and socialization, and following Maslow's Hierarchy, one typically is not overly concerned about finding love or making friends if one's physiological needs and personal safety are not in place. Once you have love in your life, that is the basis for esteem and if all elements are in place for one's physiology, safety, relationships, and esteem, then an individual can work on self-actualization to provide benefit for themselves and those around them.

Over the past few years in working with dogs, I fostered and rehabilitated hundreds of rescued dogs for our local Humane Society. Some rescues were easy and without issue; these are the dogs that were typically surrendered by their owners for reasons unrelated to the dog – the owner passed away or was sick, moving, etc. These dogs have lived their life with their basic needs being met; they have always been fed, sheltered, kept safe, kept healthy, loved, socialized, and have confidence built on that foundation and are balanced leaders in the pack of dogs I would run at any given time. The stability of these dogs did align with Maslow's Hierarchy in that their lives of consistently being provided for allowed them the self-actualization ability to contribute to the other dogs in healthy, balanced ways. However, one only truly realizes the connection to Maslow's Hierarchy of Needs through the experience of working with those dogs that come into care without having had those basic needs afforded to them in their lives up to when we met them.

These dogs come with behavioral issues like fear, aggression, distrust, disconnection, or desperation. It can just be a matter of time – along with the provision of those basic needs of the dog's physiology, safety, and love – until we bear witness to what seems to be a miraculous transformation. The

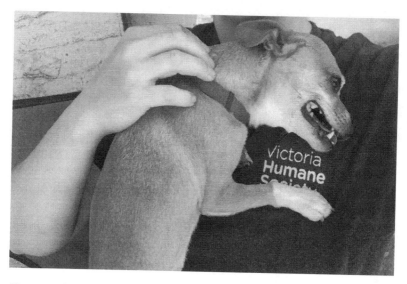

New arrival seeking comfort and assurance

challenging dogs' behavior can dramatically improve into confident and well-balanced dogs. Once the dog did not have to scavenge or fight for food. Once the dog had its medical needs addressed so it was no longer in pain. Once the dog could safely socialize and even play with other dogs that it could trust to not attack. Once the dog knew that they could trust us – the people – to provide shelter, food, water, safety, and love. Once these needs were met on a reliable and consistent basis, the dogs could finally be the wonderful companions they always had the potential to be.

I learned in our work with these dogs that our environment –
a balanced pack, consistent guidance free of unreasonable
expectations, five acres of fenced property – had the power to
be therapeutic for dogs in need of a "reset". We had dogs
come in that were completely out of whack behaviorally and
they could learn not only how to live, but to thrive. It was a
safe environment for them, with the only direction, training,
and expectation being to respect the pack. I will protect you;
you need not be scared. You need not fight; the pack is here
to help you, to heal you, to play, to love, to boost you up.
Dogs are happiest when they have all their needs provided for
- food, water, and shelter, with exercise and socialization
along with a space of their own to eat, sleep and relax as
well. If dogs never have any time on their own, they can be
overwhelmed, frustrated, and upset by the others in the
group. Happy and healthy dogs have the good measure of all
the water they can drink, enough but not too much food, a bit
of treats, exercise that fits their energy level along with
socialization with other dogs but also that safe space for

themselves - indoors - safe from the elements, predators, and other dogs. Witnessing the dog's behavior and transformations as their needs were now being satisfied is how I concluded with certainty that Maslow's Hierarchy is likely applicable to dogs as well. Dogs that came into care that had been lacking basic needs would act out to gain or protect themselves until they trusted those needs would always be available. Only after that trust was gained could the dogs positively interact socially and eventually contribute to the health and welfare of the pack in general. Dogs that were well balanced: confident, calm, and social - were imperative to the work that we did with behavior rehabilitation for the rescue and clients. Dogs can teach other dogs in ways and with greater effectiveness than I could ever hope to. That is how my perception of dogs shifted. I started to see the dogs as teachers. Teachers that were more than willing and able to share their lives, wisdom, and hearts with their species and ours. It was beyond rewarding for me to be a part of such significant and positive change in a dog's life but the greatest gift was the epiphany of the connection between the behavior of dogs and humans.

This synchronicity of our behaviors is either a result of our species' shared mutually beneficial, evolutionary history or is the reason why we could share this history – either way, it really does not matter. What matters is that, despite not linked most closely genetically, our species' are able to coexist successfully because we have an undeniable connection and understanding of one another. Yes, that is correct - *understanding of one another*. Many have sought to provide their insights into our understanding of dogs and how best to train them to be more amenable to living with humans. To teach these dogs to meet our expectations of them to be more human.

But remember the words of Madame de Staël…how often do people prefer the company of their dog to yet another meeting or social engagement?

Remember the homeless man near my old workplace, how

many of us are more comfortable assisting a dog in need rather than a human?

How many of us have our hearts bloom with the greeting we get from our dogs when we come in the door but are completely disappointed by our human family barely noticing?

Our connection allows us to understand *each other* - not just us understanding them. But we humans know best, right? Humanity has everything solved! We all get along! We always act appropriately! We never make mistakes! *(*please read those statements with heavy sarcasm and an exaggerated eye roll*).*

How egocentric are we as a species??? It seems that despite many of us losing faith in each other, we still like to dictate how other species should live with us. We train, discipline, and reward our dogs. We dictate when and where they go to the bathroom. We decide when and where and with who they exercise and socialize. We control what and when and how much they eat and drink. We even have the power to choose when and how they are medicated, vaccinated, and sometimes even killed or euthanized. We have altered our relationship with dogs, we decided we were going to do more, spend more, and be more for them. In doing so, we may love them more but we certainly do not seem to respect them as much as we once did. We are all so wise, so caring, and so patient – dogs should be nothing but grateful to have such caretakers, is what all too many people think. From what I witnessed on a daily basis, dogs are indeed grateful. Gratitude shown by dogs typically doing their very best to gain our love and approval (along with treats!). However, dogs do not always do exactly what we want nor expect. They misbehave. They make mistakes. Either we seem to take great pains to "fix" them with books, classes, training, etc. or we inflict great pain to "teach" them a lesson with punishments, discipline, or even abuse.

This is all not to say that we should not train our dogs – but rather to propose that we return to a true love of dogs in sharing a mutually beneficial relationship with them. To realize that they are dogs, and to treat and respect them as such. Let us drop our outrageous expectations of our dogs behaving like humans and appreciating them behaving like happy & healthy dogs. If truly sharing our lives with these wonderful creatures, let us recognize the lessons they can teach us about living better, more loving, and happy lives. I consider myself fortunate to have worked with so many dogs over the past few years and to make a difference in the lives of so many. I am also very fortunate to have recognized and gained insights into how dogs live, react, and behave that I have taken them as lessons to enrich my own life. From what I see, read, watch, and experience, it feels like humanity has lost its way. We seem more and more disconnected from each other, from nature, even from ourselves. Humanity seems to struggle with basic goodness – we judge more, fight more, tolerate less, cooperate less, the list goes on and on. Dogs can teach us to be better human beings, here is how…

DOG is Love

There is hope for us if we choose to learn what dogs have to teach us. Dogs show us love, they pay us attention, they seek out connection, they do not try to deceive us, they try to soothe our pain, to protect us, and never lose their excitement for the simplest of things in life. Dogs have an authenticity about them. They are so giving and do not holdback what they have to offer. Love is the greatest motivator that exists across humanity. People will sacrifice their lives - in every imaginable way - for those that they love. Love is not as easy to create as fear. It takes longer to build and must have a strong foundation of respect and trust, in addition to affection and attraction, to endure. Love takes time and effort. Fear can be instantaneous and ignorance exists without any effort at all. Worries and fears of other cultures, religions, genders, and ideologies are born from ignorance and the result is hateful actions and words. This approach does nothing but contribute to more hate. Retaliation and vengeance, war and terrorism, racial supremacy and intolerance all have the predisposition to trigger negative reactions. Those being subjected to the hate will of course want to fight for their rights and their lives along with those that support them. It is an honest reaction to lash out when someone attacks you, you want to protect yourself - human instinct is that of fight or flight. However, reacting in kind to those that hatefully assault you or others only serves to intensify the negative interactions and fuels, even provides justification of, continued hate. Remember the all too often tragic end for those dogs that answered aggression with their own aggression?

Hate is not the remedy for hate.

As a child, my favorite song to sing at school assemblies had these lyrics (these are from memory, not Google ;-)):

> *"Love is something if you give it away, give it*
> *away, give it away;*

Love is something if you give it away, you end up having more!

It's just like a magic penny, hold it tight and you won't have any;

Lend it, spend it, and you'll have so many, they'll roll all over the floor...FOR;

Love is something if you give it away, give it away, give it away;

Love is something if you give it away, you end up having more!"

There is a reason that songs sticks with me and I think that is thanks to the truth that is resonates. Like another very true adage - "Love is the answer" - it is vitally important should we, as humanity, ever truly want peace and unity. Love as a reaction to hate is the diffuser we need to employ. It is only natural. If one is burned, you run cold water over the burned skin to offset the heat. If it is dark in your room, you turn on a light to find your way. If you are feeling fatigued sitting at your desk, you simply need to get your body moving a bit to boost your energy levels. The opposites provide the balance needed - the opposite can mitigate damage. You overcome ignorance with wisdom. You overcome fear with trust and respect. You overcome hate with love.

Love is the answer and the dogs again reinforced this truth. Dogs are basically unconditional love on four legs. There is always varying degrees of intensity of that love and engagement dependent on the individual but we have been fortunate to share our lives with a few dogs that were overflowing with love. One dog in particular resonates in my memory, Tawny, a Pitbull cross. She was a tough dog to find an interested adoptive family for simply because of her appearance. She was a dark chocolate brindle which typically is not great for photographs and for people's opinions - it is a well-known fact that black dogs are typically the longest in rescue care and hardest to get adopted out. Then add to that her breed, Tawny was a dark colored Pitbull cross. Not Pitbull enough for Pitbull people to want to adopt her but too Pitbull for those nervous of the breed to take her on. However, Tawny was magic with every dog and person

Our loveable Tawny girl

she met because she was so loving. She so wanted to connect that no one could resist. Dogs that had lower tolerance levels would at first be startled with her attention and affection for them but their indifference would crumble and they would love her back like we had not seen before. Dogs that could not walk with other dogs due to reactivity, could walk without a problem with Tawny. Tawny was a blessing to have for the length of time she stayed with us because she really did help to rehabilitate a few dogs that desperately needed some safe and positive socialization with a dog that would never react or trigger aggression. If the other dog had any negative reaction to her, she would easily and quickly recognize their issue and submit to their concerns but still continue to seek that connection with them despite their initial worries about her. She was a wonder and helped to change those dogs to start to trust dogs again and actually enjoy walking and playing with other dogs. Those dogs were then happier, more relaxed, and much easier to find adoptive homes for. Tawny ended up leaving us to another foster who needed a particular type of dog given their living arrangements and she did amazing with them of course, as she was so eager to please and so good with other dogs. Finally, after months in care, she found her people and they were completely smitten with her because she was such an affectionate and attentive dog. Tawny was all love and her love improved the lives of all she encountered. Tawny proved the power of love.

Adopt an approach of love and concern, an empathy, for those that hate. What must their lives be that they have made those choices in their lives? What must be lacking in their education? In their experiences? In their hearts? Love is what is missing. By choosing to react with kindness and an attempt to understand, to offer attention and affection, you will be helping to create the change we need in this world. Love is one of those special things in life that can only grow the more it is spent, shared, and given out. We need to start spending less money, less time, less energy on that which only erodes the goodness in the world and start spending, with reckless abandon, more and more of those "magic pennies" of love.

Magic can happen in life. A soul mate is arguably that one person out there for you. "The one." The one with whom you have an instant and electric connection with; a connection that defies all time and logic since you bond so easily and quickly but also very genuinely and deeply. Soul mates are that incredible relationship that makes you feel you are so connected to another, you are a whole being when together but at the same time, you feel more complete, confident, and content in your own self. Your soul mate makes you feel like the best version of yourself. You make an incredible pair while being the individuals you always aspired to be. That soul mate connection is truly magic when it occurs. These relationships are the makings of many an engaging plot in Hollywood fairy tales and while they do exist - they are not common.

Working with rescue dogs and potential adopters, I saw the magic happen many times. When it would happen, there was simply no denying it. In talking with others experienced in rescue, they validated that it was most definitely real because they had witnessed it as well. It was much more common in the adoption circumstances of dogs than I have ever seen in human relationships. I think this was because there is less ego involved - usually - and ego can blind us, too much or too little most definitely affect whom we choose for a partner. With dog adoption, as much as some people truly seemed to be simply looking for a fashion accessory, most people want to just adopt the best dog for them. It was comical though how many people applied to adopt the wrong dog - not truly understanding themselves or the needs and personality of the dog. However, once I could meet them in person and given the fact that I had a number of dogs in my care, I could act as mutt-chmaker! After I met the potential adopters I could get a better sense of which dog was the best fit. In person, I can get a sense for the energy level and personality of the people and would often admit that the dog they had come to meet is likely not the best dog for them along with the reasons as to why I felt that way. Sometimes it was very obvious and tangible reasons, like a very high energy, untrained hundred and twenty-pound dog - likely not the best fit for a family with small children that are nervous around dogs. That is a very obvious physical reason and once explained appreciative parents were definitely open to other dogs that would better suit their families. Sometimes the reasons were more just a sense or gut feeling. I could not always pinpoint any reason beyond just that, so I still would have them meet that dog of initial interest before bringing out the dog I felt to be the fit for them to consider both options. It was always obvious, even if not easy to articulate, which dog worked best for them. These adoption matches - basically just driven by my intuition - is when magic happened. It is indeed difficult to describe because it really is just a sense that I would get, but the connection between human and dog was undeniable. Something would just click and there was an instant bond, both sides of the match were instantly in love. The dogs basically acted as if these people had been their owners forever, like they had never known anything but being part of this family. I was immediately forgotten about - no matter how much they loved me. The dogs immediately recognized the people that were for them - with that unconditional love and acceptance of the intuitive bond that was immediately established. I like to simply call it magic, that the dogs and adopters had found their soul mates. It was extremely critical if adopters already had a dog or dogs that those pets come to meet the dog that was being considered as well. Between dogs, I could also tell if there was a bond immediately or not. Dogs will immediately recognize the relationship between the two - if they will get along or not can be determined very quickly. I am not saying that they would always immediately be best friends but you can tell by reading their body language and their reactions to each other if they like each other or not, and if there is a future or not for the dogs potentially living together. As much as they may eventually get along, there was the odd occasion that there was magic between two dogs too. The best example I can use would be our own two dogs, Churchill and Mona. We adopted Mona at the same time as another of our dogs, Bumble, in late 2014. The most significant consideration in why we chose to adopt those particular dogs was their innate sense with dogs. We knew they could really help our efforts to rehabilitate dogs in need. That by adopting them, we could save so many others. They had fun with one another and got along really well. The two of them were always great dog siblings. They were always good with one another but would still seek out connections and relationships with other dogs as well.

In the summer of 2016, Churchill was a surrendered Mastiff who, because of what I can only assume was an unstable home, quickly bonded to me and refused to be adopted in the meets that I arranged for him. He would go with the potential adopters on a walk to get to know one another but upon return never wanted to stay with them. He always just attempted to return back through the gate or hide behind me. One potential adopter actually got quite angry that I would not adopt him to her given what he was telling me. I had been working on adoptions for years by this time and knew to trust my gut, especially when the dog in question was a very large and very nervous dog - that can spell disaster for the humans and the dogs. It simply was not worth it unless Churchill was confident enough to connect with them. After some discussions amongst our family, we decided to consider adopting him ourselves IF he got along with our dogs. So we had him meet our four other dogs - Teddy was fine with him, little to no interest or concern about him. Suni liked him but given her age, she was not interested in playing with him or engaging with him much. Bumble thought Churchill was great fun and they play wrestled with reckless abandon all the time. But Mona! Mona and Churchill were immediately in love with one another. It was beyond all reason the way they interacted. They would rub up against each other, lay on each other, lick and mouth each other's muzzles - they simply could not get enough of each other. So - despite their love being so over the top that we often joked that they "need to get a room" - we adopted Churchill too. I think we adopted him for the love of love really. He and Mona were simply meant to be together - so they are. We can jokingly gag and roll our eyes all we want but it is really heartwarming to see how they are together even now - a couple doggy soul mates. It is rare but it happens - that magic between two souls. When that magic would happen in the adoption meet and greets, that is when I knew I had found the family that this dog was truly meant for and that the dog would be loved and happy for the rest of its life. When the magic happened, I did not have to worry about the family returning the dog, I knew that connection meant commitment and it was awesome to know that dog would not be homeless

ever again. The same is true with human soul mates, that magic and connection is so unique and so special that it cannot be replicated or

Churchill and Mona first meet

replaced. That soul mate connection lasts even if the relationship does not for some reason. So know that your soul mate is out there somewhere, and if you are lucky you will meet them, and if you are even luckier, you will end up with them in your life. That is the kind of luck that most folks do not receive in their lives.

The majority of people in relationships are not in them because of an amazing, magical connection they instantly felt. Magic happens, but it certainly does not need to for people to be happy. A lot of money has been made by movies, books, and television shows selling the dream of fate taking the lead, of one stumbling upon and falling in love with your soul mate. Some people may have even been lucky enough to meet their soul mate but, for whatever reason, did not end up in a long-term relationship with them. Most folks are in relationships with people for all sorts of reasons that have nothing to do with an amazing, magical connection they instantly felt. For some it was convenience, others money, others comfort, others security, and - of course - many people built their loving relationship over time. It may not be some intense connection between them that instantly sparked and a bond that simply could not be denied, but it is true love nonetheless. Love that started out as interest and maybe even simply liking the other. Love that was a bit nerve-racking when unsure the feelings that were growing were mutually felt. Love that has not always been pretty or easy but it has held on despite the highs and the lows. Love that has been built on shared experiences, over years of just sticking together through the successes, challenges, pain, laughter, tears, hugs, wins, and losses. Actually, it is my humble opinion that the love exists not despite these things but rather because of them. Love that is built not just on attraction, but honest affection, attention, respect, and trust. It is all these things that create this love that may not be all romance and electricity, but is undoubtedly true because of the commitment that each partner has to the other. It was in these adoption circumstances where it was a bit tougher to know what was going to last, what was right for both the dog and the family. Sometimes the connection was refused before it even had the chance to be tried. There were times that people refused to meet a different dog simply because of its look, breed, or age. Therefore, even if I felt that we had a dog that would be a great fit for them - the adopters were not in any state to accept that option. More often than not though, it was not the people that were not in the proper state to accept or acknowledge a connection. The dogs we worked with were often challenged to connect with humans because humans had abused, neglected, or abandoned them. The dogs that were fearful or anxious were difficult to match up with an adopter (even if I **knew** that they would be a great fit). Potential adopters wanted to see that connection right away, they wanted the dogs to want them, so if the dog was fearful or anxious adopters tended to think that meant the dog did not like them and would not mesh with their family. It was hard for people to understand that these dogs who were basically enveloped in their fear were not behaving skittish because of them, but because of years of trauma. It is hard to see through that cloak of fear but I had seen under that cloak. I knew who the dog was underneath and knew that if the people just took the chance they would fall madly and deeply in love with the dog. They just had to allow time for the dog to come out from under its fears and anxieties. It would take time, but it would be more rewarding than any other pet adoption they had had. A lot of people simply could not trust that it would be okay on the other side but there were a brave few that did. Those brave few that took my descriptions and assurances into careful consideration and that were genuinely looking to not just adopt a pet but to truly rescue a dog in need. They wanted to give those dogs that most needed it, the love, care, and comfort they deserved. Those are the folks that would take the risk and adopt those fear-based dogs and sure enough, it took time but I honestly cannot recall a time that one of those fearful dogs was ever returned. A great example was a Sled dog, Porta. She was very apprehensive and had her quirks when she first came into care, but she was one of the first of her group to connect with us. She was so cute and silly. She had a little dance that she would do when feeling especially happy and playful. She would do circles and shuffle side to side. Always with the "Sleddy" (the loving epithet used for Sled dogs) smile on her face and sparkle in her eye. She would also sit and wave her paw at you with what looked to be bashfulness. She was just so endearing and entertaining. She made my heart swell whenever I walked her and her group. Her normal behavior was this playful dog with a good measure of calm and love. She was one of the most outgoing Sled dogs I had met. I was thrilled when she had adopters interested in her. The couple came to meet her and after speaking with them briefly in the parking lot about how loveable and goofy Porta was, I went to retrieve her. All of us were more than a bit surprised with the dog that I brought through the gate. Well, I am not sure if I even got her to leave the gate. We ended up doing the meet on the property to give Porta some semblance of normal. She was still very nervous and skittish. For the first awkward while, Porta was hiding or avoiding these lovely people that had come to meet her. It took time, patience, and calm. The couple were doing everything I instructed to help Porta feel more confident, to respect her needs so she could build some

Porta showing off her cute Sleddy smile

trust with them. We all ignored her, no eye contact and no facing or talking to her. We talked calmly and quietly amongst ourselves. We kept our spirits light and upbeat. We were almost out of things to talk about when Porta started to feel more comfortable. What I was very happy to see was that she was seeking the potential adopters out. Since they were not facing her, I could keep them informed of her movements and warn them not to startle if they suddenly felt a dog nose on their hand. This was not a typical meet and greet that adopters expect. This couple that came to meet Porta though were special. They were very respectful of what Porta needed and trusted what I shared with them about who she was and how to connect with her. I told them that Porta seeking them out so relatively quickly - it had not taken days or weeks - spoke volumes of the potential of a successful adoption. It was going to be difficult but with love and patience, it would be so rewarding. The couple agreed to take the chance and put in the work. It was challenging but was indeed a match for them all. Over the rest of our time running the kennel, Porta would still come to visit when her parents would go away. She was so obviously enamored with her forever mom and dad, and they were completely smitten with her. It was an adoption that lasted, despite the initial fear and uncertainty. A new family with an irreplaceable bond between them. With love and patience, a dog can blossom and build that connection a little more every day. That experience of building the bond over time made the relationship even stronger. Love that is built over time, over shared experiences, over reaching out to and for the other, over picking each other up, over celebrating one another - that love is solid. That love may not be the stuff of Hollywood blockbusters but it is the love that long-lasting, unconditional, and committed relationships are made of.

Given my love of the song and my willingness to spread those "magic pennies" of mine around, I cannot say that I was always guaranteed a return on my investment. One thing that has always been very tough for me personally is love. Not to give it but rather to receive it. To me, "love" means loyalty, providing for the well-being of the other person, sharing time and space together, caring about what is best for the other even if it is not what you would do and even if it means sacrificing for them. True love is unconditional, true love is in the little things and the big things. It is thinking about the needs and wants of the other and trying to provide for them without concern of return. There is a magic when that is reciprocated. That is long-term, committed relationships between partners, friends, and family. However, sometimes what you experience with someone, how you are treated by them, that relationship that you build with them is not based on love, even if that word is thrown around between you. Love is an action and sometimes people simply do not know how to love, they have not seen it, have not pursued it, or they do not prioritize it. The love that some people have to share is not love at all. These types of "love" are self-serving, extremely subjective, shallow, and do not last. Romantic love that is not true seems the most heartbreaking because that type of love is what people desperately pursue. The misguided women and men that mistake a fiery "love" for that they have seen in movies and other forms of fiction. However, the upside to the lack of real love in such relationships is that they are temporary and can be left behind. You can live and learn, learning as much about yourself as you do about the other person. However, the potentially devastating relationships that are not based in a pure unconditional love are familial. When one's family members lack the capacity to love unconditionally, one will struggle with knowing how to not only give but also receive love. If those who should provide for you do not, you question your worthiness. A child's esteem will suffer greatly if her/his parents do not know how to love in a healthy, unconditional way. Sometimes people are loving you the only way they know how, but that does not mean that it is real love or healthy for you or them. The funny thing is that I did not witness any unhealthy love between dogs. Yes, there was unhealthy behaviors we contended with but these were never veiled in love. The dogs were not sharing attention and affection and then harming one another. In a familial context, the mother dogs I had the pleasure of caring for all were great moms to their litters. However, what I did experience were dogs that experienced "love" that was not genuine from their human parents/owners. It was not just unhealthy - it was destructive. To listen to people who justify neglect and cruelty as simply not reality because they "love" their dogs was beyond all reason and logic. Despite science, despite their dog's poor health, despite their dog's behavior issues, they are "doing right by their dogs" because they feel they "love" them. It reminds me of abusive husbands talking about how much they love their spouse. "Love" is not always enough, or the right kind of love. Sometimes our best is not enough, sometimes we do not know better, sometimes we do not have enough to give, sometimes despite our best intentions - we fail those we love. The tragedy is that, like children, dogs are unable to defend themselves or demand better treatment. Dogs simply have to live the life that we provide for them - and given the nature of dogs - they do make the best of even the worst conditions. I recently watched yet another video about dogs being rescued from dog fighting rings and how happy and full of love they could still be. It is incredible. I did not have the opportunity to work with dogs from dog fighting rings but I did work with many dogs rescued from horrible conditions.

Lately, thanks to a documentary film recently released, there has been a paradigm shift in how people feel about and view the Sled dog industry. Given the negative exposure, the industry has fired back with a consistent message that their dogs are not house dogs and they "love" their dogs so would never do anything to harm them. However, it continues to be standard practice to have a large number of dogs, living outside year-round, on short chains, with limited attention, affection, socialization, and access to proper medical treatment. These dogs are not protected by the same laws protecting other dogs. These dogs are treated as commodities, not dogs - not sentient, intelligent, social, loving creatures. These dogs are exploited for the monetary gain and ego of their human owners. I am not writing to initiate conflict. It was my personal experience working with Sled dogs that were retired, I could tell which were cared for with a heavy hand and those that were fortunate enough to have simply been neglected. I could tell that they had been left outside their entire lives, and I could tell they were kept

Retired Sled dog, Rouge, exploring our property

tethered except for the lucky few that got to go for a run on occasion. On that note, the fact that they are excited to pull the sled does not mean that they love to do it. Any creature would be excited about any small taste of freedom from a chain. Human beings who are imprisoned enjoy getting out of their cells for a few hours every day too - it does not mean that they love prison. Sled dogs are not just tethered - which has been proven detrimental to their well-being as well as inhumane - but they are left outside year-round. With only a "dog house" (typically a steel or plastic barrel with a big hole

Soleil, from the first group of Sled dogs I cared for, getting a bath and some love

cut in one end with some straw - not a properly insulated shelter) to protect them from the conditions. Dogs die - whether from heat or from freezing temperatures, they die. Out running to the extremes they are pushed, dogs die. Just because a dog is a "working dog" does not mean that it cannot live in a home, it does not mean that they cannot be pets. No matter the age, they are dogs first. I have had these Sled dogs not want to leave the kennel building to go for a walk because they want to be inside where they are safe and comfortable. After living at our property, being able to go out and stay in as they please, playing with one another, lazing in the yard, chasing lizards, snakes, rabbits, and birds, they are not at all excited to see a harness. They do not want to have to pull anything, they have to learn that now the harness simply means more freedom to roam, hike, and explore. The initial reaction to the harness was fear. Living their lives tethered also affects their behavior. Sled dogs are spinners and pacers - on leash and out in the yard - and it is not a healthy version of exercise. It is anxiety, it is frayed

Senior retired Sled dog Walt out for a stroll

nerves, it is being on guard constantly when outdoors. That is also a result of living outside their entire lives. Being left out all day and night everyday forces these animals to be incredibly in tune with their surroundings to help assure their survival. They are always left outdoors and exposed not only to the extremes of weather but also to potential predators. These dogs, like others who are left outside all their lives, develop an extreme sensitivity to their surroundings for survival. The result of this hypersensitivity to their environment made them quite anxious and fearful when they initially came into my care. It took time for them to relax, settle, and to trust people. Once these dogs overcame their past experiences dictating their behavior, their magic would start to blossom. The Sled dogs I have met do not lose that unique sensitivity to their surroundings and the energy levels of the creatures and space around them. They can connect in almost supernatural ways to one another, other dogs, and their humans. These dogs do not need to run extreme distances in extreme weather, they do not need to be chained and left outdoors - these dogs are dogs. Dogs that love their beds, love playing with each other, love to curl up in front of the fire and cuddle while you watch Netflix.

Another unique group of dogs that was "loved" by their owner was a group discovered in a remote, forested location in the interior of British Columbia. The "mountain man dogs" were a large group of dogs that lived with a man who lives the life of a hermit and has some challenges. These dogs were riddled with odd behaviors and anxieties. They had had little human contact, arguably had not been eating a very healthy diet, and were all needing vet checks and grooming. In cooperation with another rescue and over weeks and months we had many dogs come into care. There was a bit of backlash on social media that the Humane Society was taking the man's beloved dogs away and they looked "totally fine" in the pictures. The pictures were taken from several yards away, no one could know the poor health these dogs were in simply from a picture taken at such a distance. The backlash was coming at the same time that the second group had arrived in care - all heavily matted, all intact (not spayed or neutered), all extremely fearful. Amongst this group was Lilly, she was a very sweet natured

Lilly was blind and in pain when she arrived

girl but very scared because she was blind. She had the most severe case of entropion, compounded by dehydration that I have ever seen. We did not know if Lilly even had eyeballs when she headed to the veterinarian after her group arrived. Luckily, the veterinarian was able to perform surgery to help her to regain her vision and resolve the pain she had been in for so long. So yes, I have zero doubt that the gentleman who had these dogs loved them, but it was not enough - his way of loving may have included the affection but lacked in ways that negatively affected his dogs well-being. For those people that remain critical of the rescue because that poor man lost all his dogs - he did not. The rescues did remove all the dogs to have them all cared for by a veterinarian. They were in regular communication with the owner and he chose to surrender a majority of the dogs. He did have a few favorites in his pack and those dogs went back once they were cleared by the veterinarian - having been fully examined, vaccinated, spayed or neutered, and any health issues resolved. The local rescue has maintained a positive relationship with him in order to assure the long-term well-being of both him and his remaining dogs. In the end, he did love his dogs enough to realize that it was too much to care for that many and that they could live their best lives in new homes.

Love is a powerful motivator, love can do amazing things, but ego and ignorance can affect our human ability to love. When our own issues interfere with our ability to love, it suddenly is not truly love. So while I strongly believe that love is the answer to many problems in our world - it is a true, healthy, and unconditional love that I mean. However, not all love is created equally and not all people understand how to love in a way that is a benefit to others. We need to recognize that sometimes "love" is not love, and be willing to accept that and walk away if need be for self-preservation. In relationships that you cannot simply walk away, such as familial relationships, merely recognizing that their kind of love is not healthy, knowing that the treatment you are receiving is not right, having an empathy for the limitations of the other's capacity to love are all methods through which to cope with that lacking. It can be very harmful and heartbreaking to live within a relationship that is toxic. Therefore realizing that toxicity is not yours and does not define who you are or how lovable you are, is critical to your survival and your capacity to love truly and deeply without conditions. The dogs that I worked with who grew up in such poor conditions prove that you can overcome your childhood trauma. You can develop beyond what was modelled for you by those who cared for you. You can find within yourself that capacity for true love, to care for others with empathy and adoration, to be a healthy, well-adjusted human being who gives back to family, friends and community with a helping hand and heart. Those "magic pennies" may very well be returned to you but they do not always need to be from those that you invested in.

Magic happens if you wait for it and sometimes people grow to love someone through time, experiences, and mutual interest in each other. However, not all relationships are lasting ones. There are many times we give our love to potentially the wrong person. Most of us have dated, or even lived with or married, one or two - maybe eight! ;-) - other people that we did not end up staying with. That is just natural. Yes, of course, there are sometimes very obvious and well-founded reasons to justify a split, but truly there does not have to be some sort of fallout or offense that occurs. As we grow, learn, and change, things will change for us and someone who we once liked, or even loved, falls away. Something or someone shifts and the relationship just is not the same as it once was. I would argue that when this happens we often are in denial and postpone a split until some sort of offense occurs by us or to us. That offense however, is most likely caused simply by a shift that happened but neither partner was willing to walk away then. As humans, we do not tend to read and recognize subtle signs and energy, and we certainly are not quick to admit failure. How much better would your relationships with your ex's, and maybe even others like friends and family, be if you both had acknowledged the loss of affection before either of you did wrong by the other? If you both simply accepted that you were not meant to be with each other long term? If you recognized that you each had all that you could learn or gain from being together and it was time to part? I know many of my past relationships not only would have been shorter - saving us both time - but they would have had more positive ending experiences, saving us both heartache. People cannot seem to accept the obvious or inevitable sometimes - that sometimes relationships are temporary even if they were necessary at the time they came to be. This is what I learned from dogs - that sometimes bonded pairs are just out of necessity, as a means of survival at the time or simply because circumstance forced them to live together. It does not mean that they should not have been together - on the contrary, they were together for a reason but it was not to remain bonded for the rest of their lives. From the "bonded pairs" we did see, some were even to a stage of being destructive to one another - we were lucky to have them come into care when they did so that neither were harmed. Tapping into my experience in this regard I can think of two distinct pairs that we cared for - the first was surrendered by their owner and the second was a pair of strays that had been captured together. The owner-surrendered pair were two dogs that really should not have been living together. The family had bought their first dog years before, a small Poodle cross. This calm and smart little guy ended up being a really awesome dog; social, loving, with a strong desire to please his people. When he arrived though, he was riddled with anxiety and fear, he had even started to nip and lunge at members of the family. The other dog was a young, very large Terrier cross who was very tightly wound with intense and erratic energy levels. The family had loved their little dog so much, they decided to get a second dog but opted to get a big dog. From what I could infer based on what the family told me - this second dog, the large female, was bought from a breeder that should not have been breeding. So therein was the initial challenge, the puppy they bought was from questionable sources and was not balanced from the start. Compound that with the fact that the family provided no different - appropriate for her specifically - care, training, and attention to this large unbalanced puppy than they had to their first dog. They did not provide the right guidance nor the proper amount of exercise and socialization to assist the puppy, now dog, in living harmoniously in their home. The result was an intense, no longer cute and tiny, but rather large and muscular dog behaving like an untrained and out of control puppy. The family loved the dogs but could not keep them any longer, they decided to surrender them to the Humane Society and I handled the intake. They let me know that they wanted the dogs to be kept together with me and adopted to the same family. As you can probably already guess, there were many issues I had with this request - and the biggest one, and the motivation I always adhered to, was to do what was best for the dogs. The dogs should not be kept together if that was unhealthy or dangerous for either. I completely disregarded the request but did let the family know I was going to separate the two and told them why. It was immediately apparent that the anxiety of the Poodle was in large part a reaction to the behavior and close proximity of his much larger "sister" and his anxiety only further fueled her erratic energy and acting out. They were triggering one another in a horrible cycle that was only going to end in violence from what I witnessed. So for each dog's well-being I separated them. Relieving them of the trigger that they were to each other was completely therapeutic for both dogs. The Poodle's relief was visible, his whole body relaxed and he lost that frantic state he had been in. He calmed but at the same time became playful and fun as well - he was a wonderful companion for the family that ended up adopting him not long after. He enjoyed their daughter's dog - another small, well-mannered dog that enjoyed the Poodle's company as much as the Poodle did his. It was such a great transformation and wonderful for all involved. The larger of the pair, the Terrier, took more time. She was quite reactive to the other dogs initially - regardless of their actions and energy level. Her rehabilitation took longer but honestly, she had further to go since she had never known balance in her life, she did not have that baseline already in her that she could navigate back to. In the end she did find a great adopter, an active, breed experienced family and she too, had found her dream home. These two proved that forcing a relationship is not healthy nor happy.

There was a second "bonded pair" that were not truly bonded in any permanent way. The two small dogs were found as strays, the smaller of the two weighed less than ten pounds. The larger fella was a hefty twenty pounds,

Our not-so-bonded pair,
Armstrong (above, left) and
Tarkett (right)

still small of course but he was twice as big as the little one! This bonded pair had been captured together and the first rescue that cared for the dogs kept them together. So upon transfer down to us, I thought they had to remain together. I housed them together and they both socialized and exercised with our small dog pack. It was in these pack walks I noticed the curious behavior of this "bonded pair" choosing to not have anything to do with one another. They took no issue with each other, it is not like they fought at all - but they were completely indifferent to one another and would both actively pursue being with other dogs in the pack. At the end of the walks, they did not want to be together - they would avert their eyes from the shared space and choose to separate. I always tried to respect what the dogs were "telling" me so I did not ever force them to be together, I would just let them settle in wherever they chose during their time with me. I let the Humane Society know what I was observing and it was agreed that if the dogs were not choosing to be together, they certainly were not bonded. To be clear though, the first rescue was not wrong to assume they were bonded. As I got to know these two dogs and their personalities, I could make some educated guesses as to why they had been together - they were bonded for survival. The smaller pooch, Armstrong, was a Chihuahua mix and a total social lovebug. The Terrier mix, Tarkett, was more aloof but calm and confident; he did not take any guff from the other dogs and was selective with which humans he would associate with. My assessment of the bond was that Armstrong could leverage his social abilities to obtain resources for the pair. Relying on his cute appearance and good nature he could get food scraps and even shelter on occasion. While the larger and more confident Tarkett could protect their resources, and even Tarkett, if necessary, from others street animals when need be. In the end, they both were adopted into homes that suited them as individuals quite well. Our social little Chi-mix Armstrong was welcomed into a family that had another dog that he adored and who adored him. It did not hurt that the family were big Louis Armstrong fans – it felt meant to be! The two dogs hit it off right away, playing and chasing each other around in the yard - it was adorable. Tarkett was human selective and could be standoffish so it took a few tries to find the right match. Given his typical indifference to people, we knew it was definitely the right couple when he was suddenly interested in these new people who came to meet him. He was so attentive and affectionate with them it was comical. He was so unabashedly smitten it was heartwarming and funny. He sought them out and was very insistent on back scratches and ear rubs! I knew it was a done deal when that happened.

Therefore, while bonded pairs do happen, it can be that that bond is only temporary. We need certain people in our lives at certain times, and when that time passes, we should move on. We should not force what is not true. This is further proved when one looks at people who buy or adopt dogs without any knowledge or consideration of their breed. One client family was attempting to medicate their dog into being calm because they wanted a "gentleman" of a dog. How terribly sad for this 2 year old Jack Russell Terrier! It was completely unrealistic to expect calm and quiet from a young Jack Russell Terrier and to simply turn to "medicate" his behavior was extremely upsetting. If only they had made their new dog decision based on more than simply looks. Forcing relationships between dogs or between dogs and our lifestyle does not provide for the needs of either. In these relationships, both parties are subjected to unnecessary stress, damage, and hardship. If we approach our relationships with authentic and honest consideration, along with a lack of ego that may override our acceptance that we made a mistake - we could release ourselves from such relationships.

All too often we hold on because we may not be able to articulate what has changed in the energy between the two partners, so we doubt ourselves or are too headstrong to want to admit it is over - so we stay together longer than we should. We prioritize our ego and self-doubt over our instincts. We end up hurting and being hurt - instead of just accepting the natural end of the relationship. As the saying goes, different strokes for different folks - much like someone's dream dog is someone else's nightmare - like human relationships. It is no one person's fault - it really is just like the seasons, some people only are meant to be with us for an abridged amount of time and then move on. We learn what we can from each other and about ourselves in the relationship, embrace the change and move on - ever grateful for the experience. It is much healthier for each of us and we will be much happier if we choose to remember our past relationships with a kind heart filled with gratitude for the lessons learned rather than harboring any resentment towards our partners or ourselves for the love not lasting.

You CHEWS Who You Are

Years ago, as I watched an Oprah episode she shared a valuable lesson that I have carried with me ever since. It resonates as truth across the various experiences I have had in life and the many different ways I have heard it said - "You choose who you are".

You choose. It is not all based on circumstance and what others may or may not do for you - you choose who you are. There really is no denying that a lot of our reality is based on what we make it. Our lives are a sort of self-fulfilling prophecy of what we think of ourselves and what we project out to others and how we react to the world around us. Part of that living in reality and truth is taking accountability for who you are and what you do. This relates to career and other aspects of our lives on a fairly benign level, but the intent and its truth goes to the core of your being and your life. Just making up your mind - with steadfast resolve -

seems to be all it takes to make sweeping changes in your life. If one day you decide to not smoke anymore - you don't smoke. You are going to eat healthy from now - you make those healthier choices day by day. You decide you are no longer a victim - you won't be. You are accountable for your life - do you have dreams? It is only you that can pursue them. Are you criticized for being a bully? It is only you that can choose to not bully anymore. Let's choose to spread love not fear, demonstrate concern for one another - *you choose who you are.*

In our societies, there tends to be more "takers" than "givers". This should not surprise anyone given that too often one's perceived value is based on what - money, car, jewelry, clothes, shoes - they *take* home. People are getting more selfish and focused on the material. The cost of this is a loss of love, connection, acceptance, truth, accountability, and gratitude. This loss to us is hard to measure but there is no denying it. There are so many - even those with vast material wealth - who are not happy or content because they always feel the need for something more. There is a sense of lacking, an emptiness somewhere. People search for something, anything to fill the void. The popularity of dogs and the important role they play in our lives has grown exponentially over the past decades. This is not a coincidence. Arguably, one could almost say as we have started to focus simply on dollar signs in our societies, dogs have become more necessary. While dogs may depend on humans to provide for them, dogs are truly "givers" and not "takers" in our lives. Dogs give of themselves to benefit themselves and those around them. Healthy and balanced dogs know that being together is about sharing their energy. Such a group of dogs realizes that sharing and giving of themselves helps to create a whole that is greater than the sum of its parts. The same holds true for humans, families, and communities. If we could all start to give a bit more and take a bit less, we would be shocked at how much we could all benefit. Your life could be so much better if you gave more love, respect, trust, attention, gratitude, and others the benefit of the doubt. Couple that with limiting your "taking" to taking more responsibility, greater accountability, less offense, and more time for yourself, your family and friends. By shifting our focus to giving, one can realize the magic that occurs when a group gives of themselves openly and honestly to one another - they end up receiving ever so much more in return. It seems counterintuitive but you will realize so many greater gifts in life if you choose to be a "giver" not a "taker" just like the magic penny song promised.

This truth in the power of choice of self is one I may have learned from Oprah but it was really only proven, without question, after working with all the various dogs over the years. It did not matter the size of the dog, the age, the gender, the breed - if a dog acted like prey it was treated as prey, if that dog acted as just another dog and part of the pack it was treated as such, if a dog acted aggressive it was treated like that - *without prejudice.* Just because one Labradoodle may be aggressive does not mean they all are and the pack did not bring those pre-judgments along with it to each

Labradoodle. We decide who we are and are treated accordingly. If we let our fear and anxiety define who we are, we are living in a victim or prey state of mind, which directly creates that experience for us. When we are scared despite there being nothing to be scared of, we set off alarms for others and create an unrest for all - the truth behind the morality tale of Chicken Little. This can be seen in reality when observing fear-based dogs, dogs that act like prey rather than dogs and are therefore treated like prey. A great example of this self-determination of reality and the transformation and growth that is possible through time, exercise, and socialization, is Pei Pei. This poor girl had grown up living outside, and always tethered – unable to escape other animals, abusive people and the elements. When she arrived, her behavior was the mirror of what a scared rabbit or gopher would exhibit to a pack of dogs. Pei Pei would attempt to make herself as small as possible to not be noticed or seen. She would cower as low as possible and keep her tail tucked under her so far we had no idea its look

or length. If she was indeed spotted - eye contact from dog or human - she would flee in a panic that would trigger the other dogs to chase. Don't worry! We would call them off and redirect them to actual fun. Pei Pei expected that her world was going to attack her, so she acted in that manner.

Pei Pei smiling during a quiet walk after she regained her confidence

The other dogs were not aggressive and were not predatory but her erratic and fear-motivated panicked actions drove a reaction from the pack. We had to help Pei Pei overcome

this behavioral issue so that she could start to live the life of dog, not a prey item. To initiate her rehabilitation, we offset the prey behavior by allowing her the space to feel safe. We directed the pack of dogs in directions away from her. We would divert their attention onto activities in areas away from where she was. This provided her the respect of space she needed. By allowing her that space, it created a buffer for her. She could feel in control of her surroundings and not feel that an attack would occur any moment. She started to relax. She could watch the other dogs and learn about them and their behaviors and interactions from a distance where she was comfortable. Over the next few days, we started to see her tail appear and she began to follow the pack as we moved around exploring the property out on walks. She then transformed from prey to predator, from victim to instigator - she swung from one end of the behavior spectrum to the other. She was not going to be hurt again so she was going to strike out first. She was not going to wait for a problem to happen but rather make it clear to all that she was not going to take any abuse (even when none was coming her way). She shifted from being the victim of her environment to needing to be in complete control of it and all those in it. Here is where the beauty of the balanced pack of dogs who respect one another really came into play - they let her be who she needed to be in any given moment. Aggressive behaviors and posturing were not tolerated but the pack seemed to see through it, to know that there was only insecurity behind it. She was very responsive to our lead, would instantly back down if we told her to leave it or walk away. We could have always separated her or walked her on leash - but I wanted to avoid this given her history. We - the dogs and humans - helped her by allowing her to transform into who she could be by letting her live through the process of finding herself within the balanced pack. From victim to dictator, from feelings of no control to feeling like needing complete control - the pack gave her the respect and space she needed to know she does not have to be either. She was not prey or predator but rather, with time, she learned to enjoy and flourish as a functioning member of the pack. She could run, play, get and give affection and attention. She could truly enjoy being a dog by embracing the reality that she was who she was meant to be. She was a dog, not prey or predator. The world was not out to get her but nor did it owe her anything. She found contentment and balance by being comfortable in her own skin. She was playful, enjoyed walks, and accepted and gave unconditional love once she was okay to just be Pei Pei. She stopped worrying about everyone else around, what they did or did not do.

Another example that really proved that one "chooses who they are" was provided by a wonderful little Chihuahua-mix, Junebug, who had come into foster care looking for a new family. She was an owner surrender for being "snappy". The owners worried she would bite someone. Like was so typical, the issue was not Junebug's. Junebug was not aggressive and she was not a "biter". Junebug was simply a confident little dog. However, like so many toy-size dogs she was overhandled and her "snap" was merely an attempt to be

Cute little Junebug just saying hello

allowed to control her own body. Her humans did not treat

or respect her as a dog. She was not a toy so would not

accept being treated as one. In our care, she could flourish.

Her confidence and balance were a gift to us and the other

small dogs. She was a great model for those dogs that had

little to no dog socializing experience. We found that a lot of

owners of small dogs did not typically like, or they were

complete against, their little dogs socializing and exercising

with any dogs, let alone larger dogs. There is a variety of

reasons for this but as standard practice we walked the small dogs with small dogs and the large dogs with large dogs. Junebug was fantastic with the little dog pack to help assure them that other dogs are actually enjoyable to be around. Junebug would also try to connect with any of the more nervous dogs in the pack, without triggering any reactivity or fear. She would lead a small group of them around to explore and have fun. She was one of the smallest dogs in the pack but all seemed to respect her and want to engage with her in some way. During Junebug's time with us there was one particular day we decided to maximize the amount of time the dogs could be outside by walking the two packs - small dogs and large dogs - at the same time but in different sections of the property. We had a fairly strong-willed group of large dogs at the time who were not always easy to interact with so I was to lead that walking group. All was going very well, no issues within the packs and the dogs were all just seemingly enjoying life sauntering around the property and playing or exploring. What we did not realize though was that little Junebug could squeeze under one corner of the gate that separated the fenced yard with the little dogs from the area where I was walking the large dogs. Well, imagine my surprise when I catch a glimpse of small tan creature in my peripheral vision at my feet. There is wee little Junebug! She had come to join me walking the large dogs. She was just so calm and confident walking along with us. She was not fearful at all and the other dogs treated her with the respect that she commanded with her energy and body language. She had no anxiety and she did not flee. She was just another dog out for a walk. She was seen as such and accepted as part of the pack. While she did get some odd looks and the occasional curious sniff, it truly was amazing to me how readily even the high-energy German Shepherds and Huskies accepted Junebug as just another dog and did not at all perceive her as prey. Lesson learned Junebug - thank you for really reinforcing that for me. Sometimes all it takes is an attitude shift, the manner in which you carry yourself or interact with others, but then sometimes you actually have to articulate who you are to those around you. It does not matter how you share who you are, what matters most is what you choose to be and your authentic belief in that choice. You are not what others may project onto you or expect from you. If someone calls you a bitch, that does not mean you are a bitch; if someone calls you a loser, that does not mean you are a loser; if someone calls you a leader, that does not mean you are a leader. You are who *you* choose to be. So, who do you want to be? You choose it, then you are it.

I learned and continue to learn the truth of choosing who you are. We all make decisions every day that impact who we are, what we do, where we go and the consequences of each decision made. Each choice made contributes to the end result of what we can accomplish and how others perceive us. After escaping an abusive relationship, I found strength in choosing that I was a survivor not a victim. That empowered me to take more control in my life to actually create opportunities for growth and improvement. As a survivor, my life was not dictated by others but rather by what I did and could do. I moved to a nicer neighborhood, I got my

University degree, and I was clear to not accept abusive behavior as any way to treat me. In my first job after University, I managed a team of employees. After a particularly stern staff meeting I led to address theft that had been occurring, my boss commented that I had been quite a "bitch" in the meeting. I returned to my own office and sat with that comment for a minute or two before deciding to return to his office. I confronted my boss with the insight that had it been one of my male counterparts he would have applauded the handling of the meeting as clear and decisive and his labeling me as a "bitch" was completely sexist and unacceptable. Yikes, right?!? Well, my boss was actually a very thoughtful and intelligent man and he only reflected on that note for a moment before agreeing with me. It was a lesson we both learned that evening and it led to a greater appreciation of what we both could contribute to the success of the organization.

Dogs recognize intent and are not sidelined by language - we have a tendency to try to believe words that are said but not listen to our gut instincts. There are a number of cultures, and, yes - science, that has been delving into the notion that our brain is not our only true "brain". Many believe that there is much more to human knowledge and wisdom beyond what simply occurs in the grey matter in our skulls. The idea of three minds - brain, gut and heart - has validity, and over the centuries, many have attempted to explain the truth of our knowing. We know that there is more to knowing than just logic - even in pop culture terms, we realize we are not Vulcans. We have all heard of the conscious, subconscious, and unconscious; the ego, the superego, and the id; even chakras (but those number higher than three of course). I am not prepared to tackle the subject itself but merely mention it to provide some basis for one to consider that truth and experience are not merely what we can see nor what is simply articulated in the language we speak. There is so much beyond what we can prove categorically, so much more to say and understand beyond the verbal, seeing is not necessary to believing and seeing does not always merit belief. I worked for a few years in the car sales industry and there was one gentleman that I worked with that was a real piece of work. He is one that I can honestly say, really reinforced this problem in society. He would talk to you, to customers, to bank representatives, etc. and say the words that were expected but there was always an undeniable sense of discord, a true unease. In speaking with others about interactions with this person, we all shared the same feeling of literally feeling a churning in our stomachs, like a snake coiling around in our belly. This co-worker would be saying all the things that you want to hear or expect to, however - despite the words coming out - you knew that it was not truth. It is in such moments where the saying to "trust your gut" must have come from.

The problem in our society now is that truth seems to not matter, the population eagerly accepts falsehoods simply because it is what they *want* to believe. The truth hurts, the truth is tough to take but it remains the truth whether you want it to be that way or not. However, in this day and age of spin doctoring, marketing, and conspiracy theories - along with fake news articles and organizations spreading like wildfire through social media with no filter or verification of facts. We seem to be all jumbled up as a populace with one side running from the truth and the other chasing it. It is as though words, emojis, and hashtags have more merit than actual facts in regards to everything from human rights to human history, from science to religion - if it's tweeted, shared, clicked, liked, it has more power than reality.

That is wrong, that is dangerous, and that is destructive. Working with dogs taught me that lies do not work with dogs. No matter how much you may want to believe what you are saying, a dog knows the truth. This would happen so often with people not even understanding their own dogs. I had one client attempt to convince me that their two-year-old standard Poodle did not need to be walked! Needless to say we - me and the Poodle - did not accept this as fact. Often families choosing to surrender their dogs would lie about the dogs behavior to make themselves look better or to make the dogs look better so we could take them on. I very recently

had to facilitate a surrender of a dog for a local rescue. The

owner was simply fed up with his dog's behaviors and he had

been unable to overcome them in the years of owning the

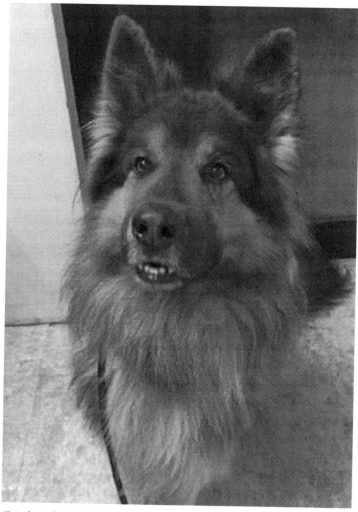

Grizzly ended up not having all the problems his owners created

dog. He told me that the dog, Grizzly, was not house trained, did not like strangers, and hated the car. In the dog's defense, the owner had experienced some terrible luck almost immediately after purchasing him and really had never truly provided for the Grizzly's needs socially, medically, and behaviorally. The dog's truth was he had very few accidents inside when he came into the rescue's care. Once Grizzly knew he would be taken out regularly on walks, he no longer emptied his bladder or bowels inside. The dog's truth was as soon as he saw me walking up the driveway he was thrilled and excited to come to me, despite never meeting me, he was more than willing to come to me and without so much as a glance back at his owner. Grizzly was perfectly fine with all people we met and encountered out for walks or at his foster's home. The dog's truth was that I could not even fully open my car door before he was pushing his way into my backseat and lay down, content and happy to start the new chapter of his life. Grizzly was more than content in the car every time I had to transport him, he willingly jumped in to the backseat and travelled without incident or upset regardless if the ride was 5 minutes or an hour. People perhaps don't intend to lie – certainly dogs do behave differently for different people – but all too often people simply project their own assumptions and issues onto their dog. The result is a stressful relationship between dog and owner that can only be healed by the human recognizing their responsibility for the dog's behavior and starting to respect and encourage the health and wellbeing of their dog.

The last story of peoples lies, or best case an egregious and seemingly purposeful misunderstanding of their dog, happened a year or so ago and it was the most hurtful - literally. A family had purchased a purebred Boston Terrier that they were surrendering, supposedly for his high energy and occasional nibbling. They had little kids and felt one could be injured. I did understand the concern that children not get bit by a dog, but in all our experience with Boston Terriers, they were all very high energy and would jump up and give little nips on your hands or clothes to engage you in some sort of connection or play. The behavior they described was very typical breed behavior for a Boston Terrier so we had no concerns accepting the surrender. However, I learned immediately that they had lied when I went to welcome and assure the dog. The dog leapt up, latched onto my finger, and proceeded to try to remove it! The owners did nothing but watch me struggle to pry his jaws open and have to grab the leash to control his continued lunges and attempts to bite me. This was NOT typical Boston Terrier behavior and, without even having to investigate the breeder, I can assure you that he was very poorly bred given his body composition and skull structure were not at all to breed standards. We did try several options for the dog but soon found out that he had a degenerative neurological issue that caused seizures and his erratic and violent behaviors. He was placed in a different foster home where they could better meet his special needs one on one. As for me, I cleaned the wounds on my finger as well as I could but given the dogs small stature, his teeth were more like needles than teeth and had penetrated the finger as deep as they could go. My finger ballooned with infection to three or four times its typical size and I found myself in Emergency requiring treatment with potent antibiotics and pain management prescriptions. The pain was torturous given the extent of nerve damage. To this day, I cannot make a normal fist with that hand, I have minimal grip strength remaining, and that finger is incredibly sensitive to the cold.

As for lies and truths between dogs, it is difficult to cite a story where a dog has lied to another in the way in which I have described we lie to one another with our words. However, a great example is not necessary in a dogs talking to another but rather in its vocalizing. Madeline was a beautiful, senior malamute mix. She came in to care in not great condition. She had been used for breeding for far too long and was having a number of medical issues, including inflamed and infected feet. It was extremely painful for her to walk and she was not shy about making noise growling and snarling - at any other dog that got too close to her when

Madeline resting during an outing when she first arrived, notice how enflamed her feet are in this photo

she arrived. She did not want to be put in any more pain so she warned the others to not run into or onto her. It took time, medication, many vet visits, and a vastly improved diet but Madeline did make a glorious recovery. She was feeling better and not in any pain from walking any longer. However, despite her acting more social and seemingly want to engage with the other dogs more she would still growl and snarl. I was concerned that she was going to initiate some sort of altercation so was extremely vigilant to monitor her and would immediately call out to her to distract if she started growling at someone. I was doing my best to prevent an issue. What nagged at me though is that it really felt different to me, even though she was indeed growling and snarling at the other dog. The epiphany I had in watching these exchanges over a few days was that her vocalizing now was playful in nature, not aggressive at all. I realized that to understand the truth of the interaction I not only needed to

Madeline feeling happy and healthy, notice her feet are now healed

pay attention to Madeline, but more importantly the other dog. When she was engaging with these dogs - even if vocalizing in a similar manner to when she first arrived - the other dogs would not retreat from her like they had previously. The other dogs were reacting to her behavior and vocalizations with play postures, happy tails, and relaxed demeanors - these dogs were not scared or threatened at all. The truth was not in the vocalizations but in the energy and the playful intent of Madeline's behavior. That is why I love dogs so much. Lies do not matter, they see your truth.

Conversely, you do not need to prove yourself to a dog, it can immediately tell if you are authentic and have good intentions. I value that as someone who has struggled over the years with insecurity, fears of not being good enough, and feeling that I had to prove myself or get external validation. Dogs do not need to know your history or experience, they do not concern themselves with what you say to them but rather the energy you create. Don't believe me? Try to catch a dog that does not want to be caught with the intent to capture in your head and heart. You will not be successful - I guarantee it. Dogs see through words you may be muttering to calm or coax them straight to your intent. If you are "trying to just grab their collar" or "slip this leash over their head" they bolt. However, if you can shift your energy and intent to simply connect with them, to share a treat or affection, you can very likely make that connection and leverage your love to a leash latch for a successful capture or corral.

The key is authentic intent rather than language alone. Unlike dogs, we seem to have lost the ability to cipher between language and actual intent or meaning. Words have such weight. So despite freedom of speech, people are losing their jobs, their integrity, and their lives over words - regardless of the intent behind those words. When did words get so powerful? We actually make fun of previous generations and the terms they used to describe visible minorities, or even worse, we demonize them for their language - this is with no real exploration of the intent or meaning behind those words. Words have weight because you give that power to them. When I was a teenager, I lived with my mother and stepfather. Unsurprising, if you have awareness of negative stereotypes of stepparents, my stepfather was not the kindest of men and had a detrimental impact on my life and self-esteem for years. One particular instance I recall occurred while we were just sitting down to supper one night and - I don't know specifically any of the discussion but I am sure we were having some words - which led to him yelling that I was a "fat bitch" and sending me to my room. Wow! Those words had power! In those days, I was already insecure. I was never skinny - so calling me fat was brutal - and girls were raised that we had to be nice to be worthy of love - so calling me a bitch was vicious, and to top it all off - he intended to hurt me, he sought to harm me and lashed out with those words. Without going into any true depth or assigning any blame, the story serves to illustrate the power of words. Those words stuck - obviously, since I recall them still - but over the years I have found peace with those words, and I actually use them regularly to describe myself now. If being fat means that I am overweight - then it is true, I am fat but I am not ashamed of that fact now. If being a bitch means that I do not just agree to get along, or that I will fight for what is right even if it creates an awkward moment or confrontation - then it is true, I am a bitch. A bitch who is actually quite proud to be someone who will do what I know or feel is right and be honest about who and why I am. In my experience, if I use the words myself, it gives me some ownership over them and I decide what they mean to me. Beyond that, the words are the same but my stepfather calling me a bitch with fire in his eyes and anger in his heart is far different from my best friend calling me a bitch with a smile on her face and love in her heart. Intention matters - words should not have the weight we afford them - it is what is in your heart when uttering the words that matter. Of course, some words have been used with such malicious intent for so long that no one who has any concern for the welfare of those of which they are speaking would ever consider using them. These words are avoided because you intend no harm. The point is we rely too heavily on language to communicate and tend to doubt or ignore other forms of communication. We give more weight to words than to intent and truth. It is odd how to some people truth does not matter. There can be mountains of scientific proof and empirical evidence of something but those same people will believe - without any validation of fact - their perception of the intent of someone's words. People hold their beliefs and opinions in higher regard than actual facts and truth. We are suddenly in an era of fake news, truth not mattering more than belief, a world where people choose to support those that tell them lies they want to hear rather than share the painful reality that exists. Apologies are everywhere - unnecessary - if your intent and heart are true. Moreover, you know the intent of words - you cannot necessarily see it or prove it - but you most definitely sense it. This is why two people may say the same words but they get different reactions from their audience. A child can say things an adult never could because they mean no harm or offense. The child is innocent. It should be like this for all - to know that or seek the intention instead of just demonizing a word. Give more weight to the heart and intention rather than the word itself at its worst, it is not always to assault. A pen can be used to write a poem, but as shown in various TV shows or movies on crime, a pen can be used to kill people, a hammer can build a house or shatter a skull. Words are the same.

Dogs recognize intent because they are not hung up on language - they communicate through body language and perceiving energy. They sense the intent of the action with one another and react accordingly. Again, puppies can get away with much more than dogs - but even amongst dogs, you see them recognizing that one wrapping their mouth around another's neck can be aggression or it can be play. That running into one another can be play, aggression, or even just an accident, and they react accordingly. A great example of this was seen in the relationship with Minerva and Joy. These two girls had been rescued from a hoarding situation and were part of a large group of dogs we fostered and rehabilitated. In the group were all sorts of dogs - various sizes, personalities, and challenges. All the dogs in the group got along fairly well but Minerva and Joy seemed to trigger each other and would get into little tiffs of sorts

fairly regularly. We were always there to supervise and they would always leave the other if we directed them elsewhere, so there

Our two sassy girls, Minerva (above) and Joy (right)

was never a major issue. Their bothering each other was purposeful. They would notice each other in the pack and one would go pester the other, would stand over the other, nip at each other - just various small annoyances to upset the other. It did not take much for one to trigger the other. However, they always recognized each other's intent. This was proven one walk when all the dogs were especially boisterous and having fun running around with one another. In the commotion, Joy accidentally ran smack into Minerva. Minerva veered around to meet the strong physical challenge of another dog. She flashed back with a snarl and teeth bared at Joy. However, she immediately recognized that Joy had no intention of running into her, especially not in any aggressive way, so Minerva dropped the show of aggression and moved along with no words needed from us to diffuse the situation. A physical push of that force could easily be aggression between the dogs but in this case, it was an honest mistake - and despite the relationship and history between Joy and Minerva, intent was the reality so there was no unnecessary reaction. The simplest of examples I can use to prove the value of intent over words is humorous. When my dogs are outside in the yard and I call them in, even if I call them hooligans, donkeys, or a**holes - they still come. There is no need to use their names or even a command, they recognize my intent and come back in the house. What dogs have taught me - throughout my life - is that truth matters and one cannot fake it for any sustainable time. I always trust a dog - if I am concerned about an interaction human or dog, I simply look at the body language of the dog perceiving the exchange and use them as my guide. So do not just believe everything you see, hear, or read without really allowing your whole self to understand the intent behind the message. Trust your gut if it is warning you that all is not as it seems. Language has too much power; we need to focus on intent - intending to help, to care, to support. We need to take responsibility for the intention of our words and actions; kindness is a magic that we should strive for. We can make significant impacts on our lives and the lives of others by simply having honest and caring intention motivating all we say and do.

PAWS-itive Reinforcement Works

Your life is a matter of your decisions and those decisions are made constantly throughout your days and nights for some reason or another. There are all sorts of reasons people do things, why people choose one option over another, or why people change and grow. All these reasons are the variety of motivations that we can use or that can happen to us that compel us in our daily lives. Our main motivations are typically to do things for money or reward, out of fear or to avoid some negative outcome, and/or for love and acceptance. Something has to drive you - sometimes that motivation is simply lack of energy or opportunity while other times it can be an altruistic striving to give back to your world.

In all aspects of our lives, discovering what motivates us or those around us is a powerful tool in achieving what we desire. Figuring out what motivates your client to purchase an item helps you to sell it to them. Knowing that your child wants a new game that is coming out helps you to get them to do more chores around the house. Realizing that you feel stronger both physically and emotionally when you exercise helps you to keep going out and exercising every day. Exploring what feeds motivations is a powerful tool for taking control of yourself and, to some degree, others. Parents use children's motivations, sellers use buyer's motivations, governments use populaces motivations - all used to encourage or discourage various thoughts and behaviors. Again, we can go back to Maslow's Hierarchy of Needs to see basic human needs as very real and necessary motivations. If you lack for security, clean water, shelter, or food, you could definitely be susceptible to being controlled simply by your need to acquire these necessities for yourself and your loved ones. It is often a cruel reality that in many regions of the world, such necessities are unavailable or very limited to the general population but remain readily available to those in power. Withholding and depriving basic life-giving resources is an all too easy way to manipulate people into doing that which they would not if they were not desperate to survive. The powers that be can create wars, incite hatred, and even inspire self-harm for eternal treasures all to sustain their power, their wealth, and their lifestyles.

Fear seems to be an excellent motivator - fear of something bad or losing something good. We witnessed the power of this motivator in the fallout of the 9/11 attacks. Because the population was afraid, that fear was leveraged to the gain of governments, intelligence agencies, and corporations who capitalized on that fear. The general population supported military measures, increased security measures at home and abroad, and allowed less privacy to be afforded to all. Our Wendell system relies on our fear of losing our freedom to maintain law and order and imprisons people for breaking the law - sometimes even when they have not. Even marketers and sales representatives use fear to make us purchase their product, "act fast or this deal will be gone" or even more distasteful - "if you truly love your family, you have to buy (this) to protect them". Personally, I have even had an advertising salesperson tell me that my electing to not purchase an ad in his magazine meant that I support pedophiles! Thank goodness, I had no fear of anyone ever believing that to be true. What a horrible thing to say and all it did was assure me that I made the right choice by not doing business with him.

Fear, it motivates initially - in those moments as a child when you were threatened with a spanking, you would stop. You stop in that moment – but did it prevent you doing wrong or making bad choices in the future? Often one will risk bad behavior despite the potential for being caught. Occasionally people will push back against authority even when it is assured that they will suffer a punishment. Fear is a temporary fix for behavior for humans and for dogs too. The best behaved dogs are not those that are beaten into submission or threatened with violence. Using fear as a motivator for training dogs has been long discredited by science yet people still resort to violence either in the heat of the moment of anger and frustration, or worse, as the standard of how to raise dogs simply because that is how their parents did it or how they have always done it. Well, to that I counter - if your parents had to use an outhouse, would you not take advantage of advances like indoor plumbing when it became available? The truth is that fear is not how you properly train dogs and it never has been. Fear is a temporary, in the moment, attempt at control but long term is not a solution as it does not prevent the misbehavior and only creates additional behavior issues around socialization, anxiety, and aggression. We often had to rehabilitate dogs who had suffered through training attempts sourced in fear. Resorting to violence and intimidation is a weakness of character and does not inspire respect and harmony from a dog. These dogs that were "untrainable" through the fear tactics their owners had used, ended up either triggering with aggressive reactions or being riddled with severe anxiety. The reactive aggression was learned as a means to protect themselves and the space around them by lashing out to create a buffer around their body. Even more damaging to the dog was fear-borne anxiety that caused the dog to completely shut down, be aloof, or disconnected from people all together. These are the dogs you will see often in shelters, these dogs are in shelters not because of what they have done but what has been done to them. Their owners broke them and threw them away like they were some sort of disposable commodity. So fear evoking, negative based training creates these broken creatures that animal rescues throughout our country have to put back together in order to safely and happily rehome them.

The tragedy with the dogs that respond in kind, the dogs that have been shown violence as the means to deal with issues and frustration, the dogs that simply reflect back the aggression shown to them - these dogs are often euthanized. The tragedy is not just that they lose their lives but there can be real potential for transformational change with these dogs. If miraculously a rescue - or an individual somehow - is able to work with these dogs, has the resources necessary for proper rehabilitation, they can be the easiest ones to have success in overcoming their behavior challenges. The behavior of the aggressive dogs has them at least engaging and taking some sort of action - not positive ones of course, but actions nonetheless. They have some level of confidence in the interactions they have and participate in some way with the events and situations in which they find themselves. Can they safely be adopted out after a couple days? NO! However, given time to learn new ways of being - I mean completely rebuilding their thought processes, rerouting their neural pathways - there is hope in a home that knows their past, has plenty of positive dog experience, and has the right personalities to properly guide and love. With aggressive dogs, there is a structure within them I could work with. The best way I can describe it, is that they write their story and I work with them to edit that story into one of balance, calm, and contentedness. Initial work with these dogs was usually one on one - just me and the dog. Depending on the dog, the interaction could be on or off leash. In these initial days of rehabilitation and one-on-one's, I could build up a bond and relationship with the dog in order to have them understand that they could trust me to care for them and keep them safe. Working in this way also served to eliminate as many variables and potential triggers as possible during the interactions. One on one, it was just the two of us to decide the energy level of our engagement, if we played or if walked quietly, it was only us. Only once that bond of trust, rooted in genuine love, support, and compassion, was established could I introduce another being to our world. That being would be dog or human, whichever was least likely to trigger a negative reaction. I never wanted to create a situation that would result in that dog ever needing to travel that neural pathway that took them to aggression. For that reason, I was extremely cautious with who these dogs were introduced to and socialized with. I could not project any concern during the interaction so that caution was always considered beforehand when deciding on next steps or meets. Over time, we would slowly progress the dog through to normal and balanced living but only after we had established that loving and trusting relationship with them. The end result, even if they were confronted with an old trigger, they would reject aggressive engagement and look to us to resolve the issue for them. I learned this most poignantly from a Pitty cross we named Boz. Boz came to us from another rescue. His owner had gone to jail and the family wanted the dog gone not just from the home but also the community. Boz was a very loving and sweet dog with most people when he arrived but could suddenly be reactive with other dogs. It seemed that

Our ever-shy guy Boz requesting I rub his belly

perhaps aggression had been expected in his life given the amount of scars on his body. Despite his reactivity, I could see the heart of a truly lovely dog. I did not want him to ever feel threatened or nervous around any other dog so I walked him solo for about the first week. A critical help to his social skills was having him neutered as soon as possible after arriving. The effects of both the surgery and the one on one attention and affection were overwhelming positive. I felt he was ready to start to socialize with other dogs, but the dogs would have to be calm and reserved or indifferent to him initially. For a day or two, I walked him with our dog Suni. She was a perfect fit for the job. Her personality was loving but never imposing or overwhelming at all. Suni was calm, confident, and never created issues with other dogs. Other benefits I felt were that she was female and the recently neutered Boz would most likely prefer that to a male. He would be less likely to trigger aggressively with a female. However, the little "challenge" we wanted to give Boz was not just to exist and socialize with another dog but a dog that was bigger than he was, which some dogs will be sensitive to. Suni was physically bigger than him but given her demeanor she was not at all threatening to him. Boz did great with Suni, he really liked her even though they did not play or roughhouse given her older age. They enjoyed walking together for a few days that really helped Boz find a sense of calm around another dog. He seemed to realize not all other dogs were going to attack him. As luck would have, a few days later, a group of Sled dogs arrived into care. These meek souls needed to be housed in the same facility as Boz so he would not have the place all to himself any longer. I was mildly concerned that the group of five, if I recall correctly, may overwhelm him but I honestly felt more excited that these dogs were going to be exactly the magic that Boz needed. Boz's energy and playfulness greatly overshadowed the combined energy of the Sleddies. They were all somewhat fearful of him initially but he showed tremendous respect for them and really seemed to thrive with the group that were taking their time to get to know him before ever engaging with him. They were together for weeks and the result was Boz could safely socialize with any dog by the time he was adopted. He loved to play, roughhouse, and chase around with other fun dogs - not limited to just the Sled dog group either. Boz helped the Sled dogs overcome their anxiety from their lives lived in the mushing industry and discover the joy and fun of being a dog. At the same time, the Sled dogs helped Boz overcome any ideas of aggression or violence that he had prior to coming to the rescue. I knew Boz had come further in his rehabilitation than I dared to dream possible while watching him during a walk with the Sleddies. He had gotten used to not just walking with them but he also liked to engage them in play when he could. It was therapeutic to both dogs until he chose to try to get Frosters - the most fearful of the group - to play with him. Frosters panicked and tried to attack Boz. When I saw Frosters react, I was terrified that Boz would relapse and we would have some injured dogs on our hands. Dogs who would be worse off than when they arrived given this altercation. The trust would be broken and we would have to start all over again. Happily though, my fear was completely unjustified. Boz was shocked by Frosters reaction. He looked at him with confusion and then chose to not react at all - Boz simply turned and walked away! Frosters started to pursue but given his fear all I had to do was call out to him and he reversed course immediately. Boz trotted over to me with a happy smile and tail, completely unfazed by the incident. It was a huge win in my books and helped to confirm that Boz was ready to take on the next chapter of his life with his new family, whoever they may be. It was in those moments, when something unexpected occurs that would have undone all the rehabilitation of the first weeks but instead was barely a blip on the dog's radar; I knew that I had made a difference in that dog's life. That I had saved them from euthanasia and could start to look for an appropriate home for him/her. Those moments showed that the dog had moved beyond the violence and was now motivated by positive aspects like socialization, attention, and affection. Positive rewards were a much stronger motivator and could overcome years of negative training if the necessary amount of time, trust, guidance, and care were provided when they were needed. Gives some validation to the old saying "You get more bees with honey than with vinegar".

The tougher cases to rehabilitate were those that were raised living in fear and that fear completely envelops their entire being. These dogs are tougher because you have to completely build them up from nothing. They are completely shut down and will refuse to take even the most limited of action or engagement in any given situation. For potential adopters who would attribute their experience with aggressive dogs as the same as what is needed for these difficult dogs, I would use my story analogy. Aggressive dogs have already written their story and just need some help editing it. The process with a fear-based dog is more difficult because they simply show up with blank sheets of paper and you are left to figure out what their story can be and how it can be written. It is more difficult to create than it is to edit - it is more difficult to bake a cake than it is to eat it. Rehabilitating a fear-based dog requires quiet and calm encouragement from both humans and other dogs to inspire that dog to learn normal dog behaviors. It is vital that these dogs move, that they run, that they explore. That was typically not happening when they arrived. They would hide in a corner, under a bush or refuse to leave their enclosure. They do not need to avoid triggers but rather discover them. The rehabilitation is doubly difficult in that you also have to provide boundaries and guidance to these dogs if they do behave undesirably - and to do so without anger or frustration, without any elevation of negative energy. Any negative reaction that is imposed upon such dogs will only result in them regressing into their fear. These dogs are extremely sensitive and will barely accept positive rewards, let alone be able to withstand any sort of a negative response from those with whom they are living and learning from. It takes copious amounts of compassionate patience.

Sometimes you cannot even get caught looking at such dogs for the first few days (or weeks). However, if you are patient, if you are authentic in your love and desire to help, you can start to break through their fear and connect with the dogs. As you can gain their trust and they are exercising and socializing with other dogs, you will start to see them emerge from their shell. The dog that came in barely able to move, completely immobilized by fear, will slowly but surely start engaging with their environment, with the other dogs, and even with the humans! I can rarely be brought to tears but having a fearful dog fall in behind me, to approach you from the "safe side", nuzzle my hand or give me a lick, has caused more than a few happy tears in my time working with them. This was how it was so often with Sled dogs. It was always a sort of magical transformation to witness as these dogs were rehabilitated. It really seemed one was watching a seed grow into a plant and finally blossom into the wonderful dog they were always meant to be.

The final type of broken these dogs could be when they

arrived as a result of fear and violence being used to train them was the hardest to overcome. These dogs were the ones that completely closed themselves off from humans. Negative, fear-based training has only taught them that they should not trust humans and that humans - even those that should love them - would hurt them, would behave irrationally, were too weak in their coping and leadership skills to be respected or followed. These dogs disconnected from humanity because they had been consistently let down by it. These dogs were left with no desire to interact with or rely on humanity for anything. They were much happier with other dogs and often seemed they would prefer to just be allowed to run on their own to fend for themselves. These dogs distrust of humans seemed to result in them rejecting their domestication and desire to be "man's best friend". This is why they are the toughest type to rehabilitate - they could see no need for me so they sought out no relationship or engagement. They need no help to socialize with other dogs and it's from the pack they derive their own joy and fun

- life's enrichment. No toys needed! No people needed! In fact, these dogs would even tend to try and sway the pack to follow them instead of me - so it could prove challenging on occasion. They are not aggressive, they are not crippled by fear, they simply want nothing to do with people. This made them almost impossible to find adopters for. Adoptive families often want a dog to choose them, as much or more, than they choose the dog. They want a dog that seeks them out, that wants to be pet, that is happy to play and walk with them - they question the adoption "fit" with a dog that could not seemingly care any less who they are. These dogs have no desire to please you, often refuse or are extremely particular on what rewards they will accept, and are independent to a fault in that they miss those opportunities to build a strong and - very literally - rewarding relationship with humans that are caring for them. It takes a very long time to build up trust with these dogs, with them rejecting you and your attempts to connect most of the time, and avoiding you often. You can start to build a doorway in the walls they have built around themselves by respecting their boundaries and seeking out those very occasional moments to present a positive reward for their connecting with you. Even if the interaction is just a coincidence really, take advantage of that moment and provide a reward. Slowly, with true commitment and respect, you will build bridges between you and the dog, a relationship that is like no other because you know this dog does not need you but rather chooses you. By far the best example of this was Willows, a beautiful Husky cross that came from another rescue we did not often work with. A rescue that perhaps lacked the proper facilities and abilities to deliver the level of care that dogs typically need. So when Willows came to us, she was already done with humanity. She was not a puppy, the veterinarian's best guess was that she was about four years old. So she had lived with someone, that someone failed her in every way - even in the rescue they chose to surrender her to. After her surrender, Miss Willows then had to endure life in that troubled rescue. It is no wonder that she was completely over humankind by

Willows out walking, actually coming to say hello

the time she came to me. She was a tough nut to crack too because she could really enjoy life with us without having much to do with us at all. She spent all her time with the other dogs. She would only come in at the end of the walk if no other dog was still out. She did not listen to me but also expected nothing from me. She did not seek out attention or affection. Even after building up a bond with her, she remained independent. She was very aloof and it took weeks to break through her walls. All of us were ecstatic when someone applied to adopt her and even more thrilled when he came to meet her and they actually hit it off. Willows seemed so happy and was looking to connect with him from the get go. It was great! He kept her for about five days and then decided he didn't have time for a dog after all. Willows came back but she was resilient and we were hopeful. A young couple with a toddler applied to adopt her. They came to meet her and wanted to adopt her. I was leery. I asked them to make sure that Willows is exactly what they want in a dog since it would devastate her to be returned. They assured me, they even got slightly offended, that they were most certainly aware of what dog they wanted and what to expect in owning a dog. Willows liked them so I chose to have faith in them despite my gut feeling and allowed them to adopt her. It was before seven in the morning the next day, when I got the phone call that they were returning her. They had the sudden realization that Willows might accidentally knock their toddler over. What if that happened near something sharp or dangerous like the stairs? Willows came back again. I was heartbroken for her and could see the toll this was taking on her. She had already cut herself off from humanity before and she started to do so again because her trust was consistently being betrayed. Then a man came to meet her and adopt her. He lived by himself, could commit all his time to her - he wanted a companion. He lived near trails and forest and wanted a dog to walk. The dream home for Willows! Until two weeks later when he called wanting his money back since she was barking too much out on the chain in his yard. What??? Chaining a dog for any length of time is not okay and specifically violated the Humane Society's adoption contract. We brought Willows back for a third time. She stayed with me for months after that - I was done taking chances on anyone that I had any reservations about. Willows being adopted and returned even one more time would break her in ways I was worried she could not successfully recover from. In those months she could rebuild her trust in me and start to hope for human companionship again. Then Willows' magic happened. A woman applied to adopt her who truly would spend every day with Willows, who was outdoors for her work every day, who could take Willows with her wherever she went, and who had a lot of dog experience. Willows seemed initially skeptical but within minutes was seeking to connect with her soon-to-be new mom. It was not easy for the two of them. Willows was still stubborn and independent but she chose to be with that woman and her mom loved, respected and appreciated her for who she was - challenges and all. Willows had finally found her forever home with someone who fully immersed her in a positive relationship. Dogs like Willows will never be naive of humans and it will very likely always take a long time of consistent positive engagement to establish a relationship with them. These dogs need to have humans that fully and wholeheartedly commit to them in order for them to trust the relationship enough to let you in. If you ever have the inclination to truly "rescue" a dog, these are the dogs that need you most. They need you more than they will ever show because they need you more than they know or will admit. It is these dogs that people often refuse to take the chance on because they do not immediately love the person. They do not shower the person with love, gratitude, and slobber at first meeting. It is these dogs that people always asked to simply foster first before they committed to adopting - which is exactly the wrong thing for these dogs that do not trust humans as reliable and stable care providers. These dogs need you to be "all in" because they most certainly can tell when you are not.

Fear based training and negative reinforcement have no positive long-term results. These dogs are "broken" by such training and I would argue humans get "broken" too when motivated through fear. If fear is your only motivation to do something, that means you do not truly want to do it. If fear is the only motivation for you to not do something, that means that you truly want to do it. Fear can mask truth but it cannot replace it. Fear will only work for as long as your fear overrides other motivators driven by your needs and wants. If you and your family are starving - that need for food is going to be a more dominant motivator than fear of being caught as a thief for stealing food or fear of getting sick from scrounging for food. Punishment does not inspire, it only serves as some sort of attempt to prevent after the fact. Punishment is, in its essence, reactive rather than proactive. You are cleaning up coffee that is already spilled, stitching up a deep wound, apologizing for spreading rumors about someone. Punishment is an attempt to change others, and will undoubtedly fail - unless the other has the desire to change. Positive rewards are more powerful motivators because they create that desire within the individual themselves to morph the behavior as a result of their internal decision-making process. Positive rewards inspire people to be better and do better despite fears they may have, rather than because of it. It is better to want to drink the coffee so much you do not dare spill that precious nectar, to have enough care with yourself to avoid being wounded, to be kind enough in your heart to not listen to rumors let alone spread them. Do not let fear motivate your life - move past it. Move past the anger, the anxiety, and the indifference that fear may have created in your past. Choose the positive. Share love, attention, and affection. Start to trust again. Pursue your dreams. Live the life you know you were meant to live once you can get out from behind the pain, negativity, and fear that have bound you until now.

In addition to choosing positive behavior with yourself, it is important to treat others with that same decency. Inflicting fear and pain on others does not yield positive long-term effects for anyone. Choosing to always blame, attack, or judge others in our society is juvenile and weak. We seem to have lost some level of maturity in our society. We lack a level of personal accountability and responsibility that previous generations seemed to possess. It may be how we are raised, our superficial connections, our more transient lives that see us leaving behind our families and communities for opportunities and adventures around the world. The end result is a shift away from community and accountability of self. If one has a problem, it often seems to be blamed on anything but that person. Dogs do not blame one another wrongly that I have ever witnessed. However, what we did see regularly in our dog rescue efforts, was people surrendering a dog, or seeking behavior rehabilitation for their dog, who completely blamed the dog. Dogs are sentient beings who have lived in tandem and at the literal pleasure and service of human beings for millennia. Now when humans lack that commitment to lead and take responsibility for themselves, their pets, and situations in which they find themselves - it is never their fault. It is somehow the dog's fault, the other people's fault, the rescues fault, etc. etc. How often in our society do tragedies occur and before anyone even has time to wrap their heads and hearts around the grief and suffering that should be felt, there is the immediate jump as to fault and assignment of blame? Why do we relish blaming others? Why do we not want to take responsibility for ourselves, our lives, our dogs? Why can we not be okay with making a mistake? Dogs with behavior issues often are simply lacking the leadership and care that their human should provide. If you do not protect your dog, it will protect itself and you. If you do not provide training and direction for your dog on appropriate behavior, they will be forced to improvise behaviors based on their instincts. If you do not take responsibility for your dog, you may lose the privilege of owning a dog and have it taken away or forced to euthanize it. We saw this so often in young dogs that were not provided the training and guidance to live harmoniously in the home with the family but the family would still blame the dog, the breed, or whomever they got the puppy from. However, to really demonstrate the fault being a human and not a dog, I will share Benji's story. Benji was a Boxer mix who had to be surrendered when his owner suddenly had to move and was unable to take him along. Benji was lovely. He was balanced, calm, and great in the house and on leash -

he was a terrific and reasonably easy dog for any family lucky enough to adopt him. A woman had been approved to adopt and came to meet him. The meet went extremely well

Always loved to see that sweet Benji smile

- Benji really connected with her and she really fell for this charming dog. I was so happy for them both until she was just getting in to her car in the drive away and just in passing, she commented she was so thrilled she had a "protector" now, she could feel safe. That bothered me but the meet had gone so well and she was already driving away that I ignored that gut instinct that something was not right. Fast forward to about two weeks later, I get word from the rescue that the woman is returning Benji for aggression. What!?!?! That dog was never aggressive! He was very mellow with all of us and in the pack. He had no history of any sort of aggression either. What happened? The woman had created that - she had put him in the position that he was expected to "protect" her. She put him in-between herself and her perceived dangers. You do not need to put that on your dog. Dogs have naturally protected humans and their property, animals, and possessions for centuries - you do not need to force them out front. If and when there is a viable threat to you, your dog will protect you as part of the pack. You cannot put your dog in the position of essentially being a weapon and then be surprised that violence is suddenly a potential outcome. Dogs need you to care for them - that includes you protecting them from dangers - including them hurting themselves or getting themselves into trouble. So she brought Benji back, I was so grateful she did. He was never aggressive when he came back. She had said that on walks, he would lunge at people and dogs while barking and growling. He never did that with me or anyone else. He was not himself for a day or two upon being returned. He was not nearly as relaxed and seemed a bit stressed, but it was not too long before he was back to normal and comfortable knowing he was safe and sound. It all worked out in the end for Benji though as a loving family, with children he was completely enamoured with, chose to adopt him. Benji was calm and happy - and the family felt blessed to share their homes and heart with their new furry family member.

I truly hope that Benji's first adopter took the time to humbly consider the insights I shared with her. That she was actually responsible for his behavior, and that she needed to change her approach and make the choice to be accountable for any dogs she may have in the future. If we do not accept blame when we should rightly own it, no one wins. Deflecting your own responsibility will only serve to isolate you, build resentments against you and you will continue to be the cause of whatever damage you are doing to someone or something. We need to start being okay with our mistakes, accepting that they are made, and committing to repairing what we can of any damage done and learning from them earnestly to avoid making them again. That will serve to build up others trust and care for you and improve you, your skills and your abilities.

Everybody and their Dog

Just like dogs running around a dog park, let's cut to the chase - humans are assholes to one another all too often. Our species' best friend, however, looks at you with love, for approval, with happiness. They seek out connection, are happy to see you, love to be with you. Regardless if you are fat, or ugly, or single, or sad, or White/Black/Asian, gay or straight - dogs make us feel love like many do not get from humans. Dogs are the epitome of unconditional love. Love based on respect, trust, and genuine concern for the welfare of others. A dog does not care what color you are, what your weight is, how much money you have, the kind of car you drive, what religion you follow, who you voted for, what your sexuality is - they just simply care for you. A dog loves and pays attention to you despite your mistakes and your flaws.

It does not matter where you live; you will find people all

around the world that love dogs. The love of dogs is somewhat universal - something that most people can connect with and understand. Yes, there are folks - of course - that for a variety of reasons, do not like dogs at all, but in general there is a genuine love of dogs across humanity. Not everyone loves and cares for their dogs in the same way. Regardless, dogs are arguably so beloved by us because they love so openly and genuinely. Dogs do not get hung up on categorizing others in some effort to, best case - understand their world or, worst case - justify hate, as we humans do. We tend to attribute other people's challenges, flaws, and failures as fault completely on them while our own shortcomings are blamed on the situation or others. Conversely, our successes are our own: our hard work, our commitment, our genius, and others gains can be cruelly attributed to dumb luck, ease, or good fortune. People will bully, mock, and confront others based on differences to make themselves feel or look better. People use stereotypes to justify their hateful words and actions. All these people that you may not agree with or perhaps even hate - these people all could have dogs that love them. We do not have to prove ourselves to a dog but we also cannot hide our intention or our truths. People with or without wealth own dogs that love them. People of all sorts of gender own dogs that love them. People from all different backgrounds own dogs that love them. All across the spectrum of people, from those that shower their dogs beyond reason with all sorts of treasures and no rules down to those dog owners that are harsh and abusive, you will find dogs still love their owners. It could be argued that dogs show this loyalty and devotion to their owners simply because that is who provides for them but my retort is seen all too often in dogs who love without being truly provided for. Dogs show incredible love and loyalty in their connections with their human companions. However, the real lesson in tolerance that dogs have to teach us is not from how they love their owners but rather by witnessing how dogs treat their own kind. I learned how to best treat my kind by seeing and experiencing the interaction between dogs. Dogs do not use another dog's appearance, nor their background, nor the collar they are wearing or how they are groomed, etc. to decide how they will treat that dog. Dogs do not have that same level of concern or focus on differences and categorization. Dogs focus on actual and true issues, not perceived or created ones. You see this in a pack of dogs; the only judgement or issues are based on unhealthy behaviors. The dogs in a balanced pack "see" beyond breed, age, size, and however else we tend to categorize each other. Granted there is the odd instance of a dog showing a dislike or distrust of a specific breed, but this is certainly not typical dog behavior. It certainly is not what I would consider healthy "balanced" dog behaviors. Dogs of all sizes, various breeds, genders, ages, and energy levels can come together as a pack. The healthiest packs - the most congenial, active, calm, balanced - was always a diverse group. In a diverse pack of dogs a balance of energy and behavior is achieved, higher energy dogs can play with each other or a number of different dogs -each seemingly taking a turn to frolic with the higher energy dog until they are tired. As a group, the pack will only react adversely to unbalanced behavior. If a dog is out of control: aggressive, overly dominant, disrespectful, that is when the pack has a problem with that dog. It is all based on individual behavior - actual behavior that occurs at that time. There is no issue unless an individual dog creates one at that time through its behavior.

Another key thing to note about any unbalanced behavior is that the pack typically helps to teach a dog balance. The balanced pack was always key to rehabilitation of any dog,

Out with the pack

for them to learn from and improve themselves. A pack could teach the dog to trust again, to play, to be curious, to be respectful of other dogs and people. It was amazing to see and very rewarding to be a part of such transformations. That an individual could find a new and improved, confident self by simply sharing space and learning lessons from a diverse group of balanced individuals. The pack did not all react the same way to the individual - some would ignore, some would correct, some would chase, some would try to play - each member of the pack would try to connect with the unbalanced dog in a way that was comfortable and natural to them. The pack also did not seem at all concerned with how each of their group chose to interact with the unbalanced dog. It is not like the pack would be upset by the action or inaction of one another, they did not use that against them, but all simply seemed to understand they exist together and are stronger together. There was no consequence if one dog ignored while another corrected - the pack made what they needed to work. It is like this in a strong human family; each family member loves and respects one another despite their own individuality. If one family member's behavior is out of line, the family steps in to try to resolve or prevent the unwanted behavior. Each family member will most likely have a different approach - mom may choose to comfort, dad may yell, sibling may ignore, grandpa may share a story from his youth, and grandma may make their favorite meal and then yank on their ear with a threat of curses! All have their own ways to approach their family member who is acting inappropriately but all are valid and likely all have a piece of the whole solution to working through and beyond the issue. Each family member addresses the behavior in a unique way but all from a place of love and simply a desire for the unbalanced to stop. Dogs are social creatures, just like us. Dog packs are like human families. Dogs are excellent at being together in a balanced pack because that balance comes from diversity with respect afforded to each individual. A healthy balance is achieved through the respect the dogs show one another to allow each to be their own dog as long as that dog is respectful of others in return. This respect creates trust. Trust that none will harm another, so the individual can feel safe. Once a respect and trust is built, then the dogs could truly play, connect with, and care for one another. It is when one tries to impose itself on another who is unwilling that issues can arise because it is a violation of trust and respect so care and concern are obviously lacking. Dogs do tend to have a "live and let live" attitude towards one another and that is a healthy attitude for us to adopt as well. We need to respect each other, to create and build trust amongst each other so that we can feel confident in opening our hearts to one another. We need to feel secure in caring for and being vulnerable with each other, as that is where genuine concern and unconditional love is cultivated.

We need to offer the foundations of unconditional love to more than just ourselves and those closest to us. We have to respect, accept, and love others for who they are - even if they are somehow different from us. This is how people can learn to trust one another and truly benefit from diversity.

The other option - sameness - provides us with only limited potential with long-term negative outcomes. There is a weakness in sameness. Diversity is where strength and longevity exists. There is so much evidence of this yet, you still find people that do not want to include others of various races, genders, religions, and cultures in their work, school, or community. Diversity creates evolution; if we did not adapt or change we would not survive as a species. Diversity allows for innovation, having a wide assortment of experiences and teachings from which to draw on for inspiration in how to improve processes, products, and people. Diversity provides protection, by having multiple methods to solve a problem, multiple sources of resources, multiple strategies, means that you can choose the best option or that if one option fails there are others to fall back on. Diversity results in strength - strength built on continuous success and improvement best protected from ongoing changes or unexpected occurrences. Everyone has heard of diversifying your "portfolio" if you choose to invest in the stock market as the most obvious example of strength in diversity. Another well-known, common knowledge example is seen in dogs. When looking at the long-term health and well-being of a dog, often mixed breed dogs are healthier as they have less chance of falling victim to those illnesses and diseases that are prevalent in a particular breed. Of course, I am not talking only of inbreeding and poor breeding but particular breeds' predisposition for certain ailments. One quick Google search of "dog breed specific health problems" results in over a million links to explore further. Examples like Bulldogs having respiratory issues, Pugs having chronic eye problems, German Shepherds having hip dysplasia, the list goes on and on. I am not saying that mixed-breed dogs do not experience health issues, of course they do! We all have our own unique health issues. It is just a well-known example where diversity creates a strength. However, in regards to behaviors and healthy socialization, diversity again shows to be superior to similarity. The most content, relaxed, and joyful packs were those that had a blend of activity levels, breeds, and ages. The more active dogs were a source of entertainment and inspiration to play for the less energetic dogs. The calmer dogs demonstrated the positive aspects of stillness and exploration of one's environment to the higher energy or younger dogs. It was from the dogs that were not the same that a dog would learn improved behaviors, discover new activities, and share attention and affection. In dog packs that I have run with having too much of one breed, one energy level, or one gender made a noticeably unbalanced and unsettled group. If you have too many dogs of similar ilk they upset the balance of the pack which can result in chaos of reactivity, fear, or discord. We learned this from our work with retired Sled dogs. We would usually receive a group into care at a time. Given the lives these dogs had endured prior to coming in to our care they were riddled with a whole host of behavioral challenges. Each of them had a varying degree of health, fear, and social abilities. Given their typical tolerance of one another and the intense fear that some had of other dogs, we did start them out as their own pack when they came into care. They would run and play, they enjoyed snuggling up on a cozy blanket inside, and would naturally follow one another around. Working with them as a pack allowed us to manage those in the group that were the most fearful. Often these dogs were so fearful of humans you could not face them nor make eye contact without them

A couple of retired Sled dogs having some fun with a happy go lucky younger pup

fleeing from you. It would have been practically impossible to work with these types of dogs without the help of the others. The more confident dogs acted as a bridge. They would follow us and make connections. If we were there to take all the dogs out for some exercise, the fearful dogs would not have left the building unless we were completely out of the way and they could follow another more confident dog. The physical management aside, the more confident dogs would bond with us and that provided an emotional and psychological bridge for the fear-based members of the pack. I would equate those connections with the confident dogs to references on a resume. The fearful dogs would watch our interactions with the others and assess us over time. Eventually they would surprise you by starting to trust you and seeking out connections with you. So the unbalanced dogs were greatly benefited by the relationship and influence of the confident dogs in the group. However, we noticed that if we simply left all the "Sleddies" together and never introduced them the pack in general they never seemed to realize their potential confidence, happiness, and enjoyment of life. Even the more confident dogs in the group lingered in fear, too easily unnerved by the smallest of triggers, and found it especially challenging to overcome their inability to

reasonably handle the unexpected in their surroundings.

Change was a challenge and normal day-to-day, normal

Just a couple friends having fun without any fear

house things, would surprisingly terrify these dogs that had

never seen such things before. A ceiling fan could trigger

panic. A doorway could be nerve wracking. A car driving

by could cause a total shutdown. This is the problem of

sameness, of limiting one to only one dimension in their

group. These retired Sled dogs could realize some great

moments of rehabilitation but they would never grow beyond the most confident in their pack. Certain days and situations even the most confident could easily backslide into fear if the others were all influencing at once. Once I realized that the more confident individuals in the group were not benefiting from the pack, perhaps even being negatively affected by them, I chose to move them into the main pack. Once they joined this more diverse group of dogs they could fully realize their potential. They would find greater confidence and balance in their energy between calm and playful that best fit them as an individual. They became less fearful as they could use the diverse group as a way of understanding the world around and occurrences in it. By being part of a more diverse group they could best find and develop into who they were as a dog. They did not need to live in a fear "bubble" for survival. The other dogs could teach them and interact with them in ways that other Sled dogs could not and that I certainly never could. It was our most valuable rehabilitation tool - our balanced and diverse pack of dogs.

Over time, as each Sled dog became more confident and able to do so, they would join the main pack to continue to improve their health and enjoyment of their lives. Sameness is comfortable, it can be easy - not hard to understand others when you are all the same. Sameness is often supported by fear and ignorance - fear of change and the unknown is leveraged against any suggestion of diversity, fueled by ignorance of differences, of reality, and of potential benefits. However, diversity allows an individual to realize new ways of thinking, of improving, and of living that one can choose to adopt if they see that it will benefit them. Diversity simply puts more tools in your toolbox so to speak. With the global uptick of urbanization, one can be easily overwhelmed by just the thought of making connections and building a sense of community with those that are unlike them in some way. It is unreasonable to expect a person living in New York City to know all the other New Yorkers. However, why not establish a network within one's neighborhood, block, or even just their apartment building. Try to make connections with those you see every day, those that are physically present in your life. Hold a door open, share a smile when you make eye contact, offer help when you see a need. Build relationships with those you share space with. Instead, we tend to build our connections with those that are very like us - people with similar traits and beliefs join Facebook groups or start organizations or clubs to support that one thing we share in common. This shifts community into a singular notion rather than diverse group of individuals that we would have to learn to share space and time with despite potentially significant differences of opinion and belief. That is what made us better and more tolerant people in previous generations. That diversity within a community rather than polarizing ourselves into groups on one side or the other of some divisive issue or belief. When we surround ourselves with like minds, then we can easily justify our actions and choices because we will be supported by those we have selected for our circle. Those that are comfortable and easy, not challenging, and it feels good because it feeds one's ego as well as our desire for acceptance. Diversity may not be as comfortable or easy for people, but its value is worth any challenges one may face to participate in it. Choosing tolerance will not only benefit others but will certainly enrich your own life beyond your expectation and much to your pleasant surprise.

Diversity does not preclude consideration for the individual, quite the opposite. Each individual in a diverse group should be at the very least respected if not loved. Dogs proved this to me all too regularly. The saying really should be "to thine own dog be true!" Over the years, we have had the pleasure to meet and care for all sorts of dogs. Many dogs are the playful, loving companion animals that most people think a dog is. However, each dog is unique and some have more idiosyncrasies than others do. Some dogs you cannot make eye contact with, some dogs almost physically burst from their high level of energy, and some dogs are just a little weird. :-) Dogs all have those little quirks and traits that make them who they are. Some have a few more than others.

For those that I would often describe as simply having a bit more personality, it could be a challenge to find a friend for in the pack or to find a family for if we were fostering them. The challenge was not to love them, we always did. Rather, the challenge was really about what was best for the dog and to find that match for the puzzle piece that they happened to be. A great example of this would be two particularly unique dogs that were regular guests of ours. Both Bentley and Zuzu had been clients of the kennel that operated before we took over. We defaulted into their business somewhat but most

Bentley following me through the orchard

definitely we earned our place in each other's hearts. I met Bentley first, not too long after taking over the business. His mom was concerned about the change in care - the dogs being off leash, exercising and socializing with us as a group. Bentley could be reactive, he could be anxious, and he could just be weird in unpredictable ways at home or out on walks. I told her to just bring Bentley to meet me and then we would simply go from there after seeing how it went and how he was. I met them out in the parking lot and did not even look at him. I simply walked beside his mom for a short bit and then had her uneventfully hand me the leash and keep walking. It was only a minute of two but Bentley was completely disarmed - curiosity seemed to override any fear or anxiety that he may have thought to have. His mom and I stood beside each other just chatting and ignoring him further and he approached me for some attention and affection. His mom was shocked! He was never okay with new people, how did I do that? Needless to say, Bentley became a regular visitor and even though we have moved away, he still holds a piece of my heart. We used to joke that Bentley was my boyfriend; we were simply smitten with each other. However, while we shared an affection, generally, Bentley could take or leave the pack and they felt the same of him. There was never an issue but Bentley was only following me around the property out on walks, not the dogs. That was until he met Zuzu. The first time Zuzu came to stay her dad was a puddle of nerves about the kennel having a new owner and new ways of caring. Zuzu could be reactive with people; he was worried she would attack me. He even asked me to not to engage with her at all. He insisted that he put her in her enclosure - one furthest away from all other dogs - and that I not try to pet her or walk her. She only stayed one night, I balanced his care requests with Zuzus needs and my own safety but still had to open the door in her enclosure that allowed her outdoors and of course had to feed, water, and clean. That first visit went quite well, especially considering her owner's concerns. I was not afraid of Zuzu, I felt sorry for her. As her dad and I got to know each other, he shared how he felt guilty that changes in his life had altered her care, coupled with his own anxieties, had adversely affected Zuzu. She had once been a happy go lucky puppy that was more than happy to go to a dog park. Now she was not really that

Zuzu being goofy and having some fun jumping around

happy about anything. I asked her owner if I could try to help her rehabilitate a bit back to that dog she once was during her stays with us. He agreed without any hesitation - he felt sorry for her too. It took time - many visits over months and months - but I worked to transform Zuzu a little bit every time. I went from having to be concerned about her potentially biting me, to welcoming a dog that was actually happy to see me when she came to stay. She regained some confidence and trust to become a happier, more social dog, while retaining just the perfect amount of quirk to her. I should maybe qualify my description of "more social dog". She went from reactive to tolerant, if not aloof. She would not start any problems or seek out conflict with anyone, but she also did not seek out play or companionship either. That is until a fateful stay when both Bentley and Zuzu were guests of our establishment at the same time. I had known these dogs long enough to know what to expect from them. Except when I did not. I have no real explanation for it, but Zuzu and Bentley found their matching puzzle piece in one another. These two dogs that never even seemed to look at other dogs were playing with each other, chasing around, rubbing up to each other, and following each other around - both pretty much completely forgetting I existed! It brought a tear to my eye - I was so moved with joy that these two dogs, who had never really had anyone but me previously, had found one another. They were so happy to have found one another.

Dogs do not worry about differences. Dogs let their freak flag fly! They know they can be themselves without concern of judgment or hatred from other dogs. Dogs are less stressed in packs because of the benefits of social connections but also because of the acceptance of the group of each individual. Dogs know they will find other freaks like them to enjoy life with but in the meantime, they can be confident that they will be accepted without judgment. Why can humans not do this? It seems just so basic and beyond reasonable. Just imagine how much more peaceful the world would be if we could all be this way. If we simply accepted and were kind to those we think are quirky, odd, or weird rather than change them or judge them. They would be happier, and so would we.

Generalities about breed - like human stereotypes - may have some underlying truths but there are also many exceptions to the "rules". Individuals are certainly more complex than any stereotype applied to or judgment made about them. People have universal truths and needs that connect all of humanity and our diversity of traits can be loved and valued, they do not have to be hated. Dogs are amazingly accepting of all sorts of what humanity sees as differences. Dogs do not typically take issue with differences that many people elect to create conflict and discord over. One's sexuality is one of those traits that humanity chooses to focus on as a reason to hate, judge, and demonize. Of late, there has been much discussion and debate surrounding the LGBTQ (Lesbian, Gay, Bisexual, Transgender, and Queer) community, gender fluidity, identity, and rights. Often the discussions are amongst folks that have little to no actual stake or connection to the community itself. On the contrary, these individuals/groups merely have a negative opinion of that sexuality based on their individual beliefs rather than actual facts about those that they are attacking or any connection to individuals who identify with the LGBTQ community. This is one of those divisions, created by humans, that has no bearing on one another's value - being gay does not make someone good or bad, just like being straight does not make one good or bad. Who we are is well beyond our sexuality and our acceptance of one another should not be defined or confined by it. We all know that dogs will love their human regardless of their gender. However, I have witnessed that dogs are amazingly not just accepting of sexuality humans, but also in other dogs. It is not my intent to be overly controversial, but I know that there can be gender fluidity in dogs simply from my experiences with such a number of dogs that were able to freely interact as they pleased. We most definitely did not allow dogs to disrespect one another by invading their space or imposing their will on another. As such, most often we would intervene if one dog decided to mount or otherwise engage in some sort of sexual behavior since it can be a type of intimidation or domination of one over the other. The dog being pursued or mounted was typically an unwilling participant in the act so we would step in and prevent any ongoing advances. By allowing each dog to simply be themselves, without fear of having other's will forced upon them, allowed for healthy and happy packs of dogs. Occasionally though, we would find that the dogs engaging in such behaviors were equally interested in initiating the acts. Both dogs were consenting participants in their interactions, the play was not actual intercourse but excited, arguably, sexually based actions like mounting, humping, licking, etc. They each would take turns initiating and pursuing each other to engage in what they were enjoying doing with one another. It did not seem to matter if the dogs were male and female, both males, both females, or even a small group of whatever mix of sexes - they sought out one another to engage in that manner. In those instances, when all involved not only showed the desire to engage with one another but found enjoyment doing so - we, and the pack, let them be. These "gay-nines" simply enjoyed each other in a particular way that not all dogs shared with them. They did not force themselves on other dogs that were not interested. They respected the pack and the pack respected them. The rest of the pack did not attack them, they were not threatened by their behavior, and they certainly did not feel any need to try to prevent them from engaging with one another. They also did not try to block them from enjoying other types of play with whoever nor deny them entry into the kennel at the end of the walk nor did they worry about which tree they decided to pee on - it was all a non-issue. Dogs simply accept each other, as a rule, as each other is - the only issues that arise is in those times that one dog does not respect the other. To be clear, the "disrespect" with which dogs take issue is not something imagined or perceived and simply projected onto another dog - it is a physical act or interaction imposed upon one dog by another. One dog simply being interested in playing with another dog in a particular way that they both enjoy does not constitute disrespect and does not elicit a reaction from the pack. The dog pack simply was not hung up on the same things that we humans do.

I completely understand that simply sharing my observations of these dogs in this particular way will upset certain people. That some will even argue that mounting does not mean a dog is gay and that this mutual pleasure seeking, regardless of gender does not happen. Well, number one - get over it, my experiences need not have any effect on you. Number two - I am well aware that not all mounting is even sexual let alone equates to any labeling of sexuality but it is the position in which dogs copulate. Number three - it does happen, it happens when dogs are free to just be themselves and most often that does not occur in this day and age. If I take my dogs to the dog park, the other pet parents are not going to be comfortable with their dogs mounting mine nor my dogs mounting theirs. As a rule, we humans are not as accepting as dogs. We tend to be overly neurotic about sexuality and gender despite the advancements in LGBTQ rights in our society and the politically correct acceptance of one's identity. People may try to justify their biases against non-heterosexual relationships through interpretations of their religion or citing negative stereotypes and falsehoods but there is simply no true reason to hate or judge others based on just one aspect of their individuality. Especially when the reality is that, that aspect does not even affect who you are and your life. Again, diversity does not always mean everyone will feel comfortable but it will open up your life and experience to a greater understanding of humanity and allow you to be a better person.

Dogs that are disrespectful, unbalanced or aggressive are avoided or corrected by the other dogs - but all others are accepted. Different ages, different sizes, different energy levels, different breeds, different colors all can make up a wonderful pack of dogs who enjoy sharing experiences with one another. New dogs are welcomed into the pack after basic assessments of energy and personality based on body language and smells. Even dogs that were initially out of balance or control are immediately accepted once they mitigate their issues; on their own or with the guidance of strong, calm, and confident pack members. The pack do not hold on to previous mistakes or insults that the dog may have made. They live very much in the present and approach life and existence with acceptance.

A great example of this is Cobb. Cobb came to us as a foster from a remote community where he had been a stray. In his life prior to being rescued, he would have had to fend for himself for food, water, and shelter. Given his behavior during initial assessment, I can guarantee his existence had not been easy and he often would have had to literally fight to survive. He was very particular about who he shared space with, he had over the top reactions to any perceived infractions, he did not trust the other dogs and he did not trust that he would be provided for. Cobb did not feel well either, for whatever reason - the neglect or the food - he had a horrible skin infection that affected his mobility and his

Cobb feeling happy and so much better after getting proper nutrition and medical care

mood. We initially thought he was a senior dog, due to how restricted his movements were and his stiff gait, until the medications and proper nutrition provided recovery and relief to his body. Once he was feeling better - better mobility, less pain, and happier, even playful demeanor - we re-introduced him to the other dogs. It took time, it took guidance, and it took some amazing - calm, well-balanced, non-reactive - dogs but Cobb ended up being a very loveable and engaging dog. Once he knew the other dogs were not going to mess with him, he relaxed and opened up his heart and spirit to the group. With dogs and humans alike Cobb would make connections and show attention and affection. He even won over his forever family - who really did not want a super fluffy, furry dog, that is until they met Cobb. With Cobb they found magic despite the initial resistance based on his physical size and fur factor. It is just one example, of many I experienced, where people dismissed dogs based on biases they held against a breed, size, or age - only to realize that true magic exists in letting go of those prejudices. Cobb was a success story across the board. He overcame his own insecurities and reactivity through rehabilitation by the same dogs he initially attempted to engage with aggressively. Cobb became a valuable part of the pack, as he shared respect, trust, attention and affection with all. In the end, he was adopted by people that had initially refused to even meet him based on biases that do not truly define a dog - nor a person's - values, merit, spirit, or personality. On the other side of their biases, they found a dog that became a family member; they found love; they found magic.

The funny thing about tolerance in our society is that even those that say they value it, can sometimes be the least tolerant, accepting, or forgiving of others. Like some sort of virus - transmitted through the media and social media - hatred is rampant in this day and age. Radical means are being taken to further ideological and religious beliefs. While not the necessary intention of the Bible, the Quran, etc there are many who are using religion and their own suffering as excuses for harming, even killing, others. Political ideals are also being used to polarize differences and create discord in our society. It feels dangerous to lose sight of the fact that we all have the same needs, the same seeking for acceptance, love and happiness, while we are caught up in greed, ignorance, and ego. The enlightenment of a society to value acceptance and equality cannot and should not be forced.

Enlightenment - if we look at Maslow's Hierarchy of Needs - is part of self-actualization. As such, it can only be achieved when and if all others needs are met with consistency. So while there are people who lack homes, water, food, love, and other needs, they cannot realize that self-actualization. Forcing enlightenment onto an individual is simply not possible. This is where hate and ignorance can be born - if tolerance and caring are expected or forced there is no authenticity to it. Empty words lead to only surface or facade changes without true shifts. Forcing change upon someone make them feel attacked and justifies them considering themselves the victim - even if they truly are not. The political correctness of our society only served to push people's fears and ignorance underground. There is merit in leading by example yes, but true change of millions of people does not happen immediately and does not happen through osmosis. As a whole, even the political correctness within our society has gone overboard. We have lost sight of intent - yes, words do matter and have power - but it seems that even a comment made in jest or without venom is deemed egregious beyond all matter of reason and the speaker of those words is vilified and must beg forgiveness. To have this unbalanced approach gives footholds for those that live with hate in their hearts. It begets sentiments of "no pleasing the masses!" People retaliate with feelings that it does not matter what you do or what others have accomplished. It turns those who society deems as villains for using certain words into martyrs and victims. The intention of equality and tolerance is to not demonize anyone - to embrace all, empower, and build up. However, so often due to fear, ignorance, and ego even those that preach tolerance and love will attack those that are reasonably innocent of that offense they have perceivably committed. When one group goes overboard to attack someone, regardless of the offense, that individual becomes a victim of that group and a martyr, or even a hero, to those that share his/her same belief. In truth, that person is not a victim, a martyr, nor a hero but simply a human being. When we demonize people for sharing their beliefs - right or wrong in our opinion or in light of facts - how can we possibly hope for discussion? We need a dialogue for the exchange of ideas and facts to allow for education, growth, and advancement. If a child exclaims that two plus two equals five, is it in anyone's best interest to drag that child out in front of the entire school and force the child to apologize for saying five and then remove him from class and school? Accompanied, of course, by relentless chiding and abuse from the other students? Does that seem right? No, it is obviously ridiculous. Is it not better to allow for open exchange of ideas, without the vicious attacks from either side? So much more can be accomplished through simply exchanging ideas, relating experiences, and truly trying to understand and educate one another. That is the value of tolerance as it improves the lives and experiences of all. We have too much information at our fingertips nowadays, or rather too much misinformation. We get caught up in projecting ourselves and our judgments on one another. We leap to conclusions and rush to lash out at those that have committed the offense we think they have. Dogs do not do this - it was always surprising to me that dogs seemed to sense exactly how much counter to provide against a slight or an offense of another dog. Perhaps this is because they are not preoccupied with words and their meanings but rather seem to use energy coupled with body language to understand those around them. If a dog lashed out or was unbalanced, there was always the chance that another dog would counter them - but it was extremely rare that this ever went over the top. Those couple of occasions it seemed to go too far, a dog could trigger multiple dogs at once - like can occur in our social media - the instigator would quickly become the victim when the others collectively react. However, not much can be learned by any dog in that scenario. It was quickly broken up and the dogs separated but nothing was gained in the long run. There was no rehabilitation possible in this theatre of aggression. The amazing transformations and the learnings that occurred in the rehabilitation for those dogs that required it, happened over time and not through a fight. Some of the dogs in the pack would stand up for themselves if necessary but the surprising and effective means of countering was an even and measured response. When a dog would act out against a member of the pack, that balanced dog would not only defend itself but would counter, and often overpower, but never get to the point of hurting or injuring the other. The balanced dogs would counter, would fend off, grab hold of, and even pin down an offender - with their paws and their jaws. However, these dogs left no mark or injury on the instigator besides perhaps a bit of bruised pride. They would walk away once the situation diffused and the initial aggressor relaxed. Those moments did not seem to have to be repeated often, if ever again. The most common occasion I had to witness these scenarios was the all too common surrender of young dogs that were not ever trained to stop "puppy" behaviors. It is almost an epidemic of how many people buy or adopt puppies and then do absolutely nothing to guide or train them. These puppies grow into dogs that are out of control and lack any self-regulation. Remember Cobb? Our Norwegian Elkhound or Husky cross who was initially a bit reactive with the pack. He was in care for quite awhile and had become a wonderful, calm, and confident leader in our pack of dogs, when Neville arrived. Neville was surrendered to another rescue we were partnered with up north. His owner had moved on and left this untrained dog with his, now ex-girlfriend. She wanted nothing do with the poor pup so luckily we got him. Neville was a very large, some sort of Hound mix, no-longer puppy who lacked any sense of others personal space and manners. We seemed to constantly be correcting and redirecting Neville from jumping on us and other dogs, from mouthing and snapping - it was in play but still not appropriate. This dog had been provided no sort of guidance in his young life. He truly was out of control without an ounce of aggression but erratic enough that others were put off by him. His size and intense energy level made him extremely overwhelming to many. At first, the pack tried to simply ignore the disrespectful

Neville was a happy, hyperactive, handful!

behavior but their patience ran thin as Neville was not dog

savvy enough to understand any body language or cues the

others were giving him. It was only the second or third walk when Cobb decided something had to be done to address Neville's behavior. Neville had somewhat fixated on Cobb from his initial meeting of the pack and would pester him as consistently as possible with us continuously attempting to redirect him. It was the late afternoon walk if I recall correctly and, as usual, Neville was tearing through the property and pack with reckless abandon and with no respect for anything or anyone. That is until Neville jumped on Cobb. It was only a second, or mere fractions of one, before Cobb had flipped Neville off of him and onto the ground. Neville lay under Cobb, belly up, and crying for help. I was stunned at the speed of the reaction and was worried for Neville until I could see that Cobb was not hurting the young dog in any way. Cobb had overpowered him. Cobb was a big dog and had great dog understanding. Neville was indeed crying but Cobb simply was holding him down - and only with his paws, not his jaws. He was holding him down and staring hard into his eyes - it was a moment of teaching boundaries and respect. I allowed Cobb to linger for a few seconds in hopes the lesson would be learned and then called

him to join us as we walked the other direction. Neville had

not been aggressive but his play was not healthy, he needed

to learn how to engage without forcing himself onto others.

He did not need a violent reaction and he did not get one - he

got a firm reaction that properly countered his own action.

He forced himself on to others so the counter Cobb utilized

was to force himself on to Neville. He demonstrated to

Neville that it not only does not feel good to be disrespected

but also that Cobb could force his will on to Neville if and

when he wanted. Those are powerful teaching moments -

when you can demonstrate your ability to do some sort of

harm against someone, yet you choose to not - even if they

began the altercation. When you can show that you have the

power to overtake, to harm, or otherwise best the other and

you elect to save that soul instead - that is what makes

heroes, that is what makes leaders, that is what creates trust

amongst a group of varied individuals. In a well-balanced

pack of dogs there is typically little to no conflict. Even

behaviors that can be taken offensively – mounting, knocking into, jumping on – are simply blips on the dog's radar and have reactions from completely ignoring it to countering in even measure. There is no over the top or out of control reactions to others mistakes or missteps. Most often, a dispute or fight can be avoided by just by walking away. That inspires people, that moves people, and that changes people's negative opinions of one another - to go above that which is expected. As Michelle Obama said "When they go low, we go high".

Life BITES Sometimes

Despite our best intentions, life can be ruthless. We experience challenge, injury, and loss. In our lives, we have all experienced pain and we will again. Pain is a vicious thing. Pain comes in all sorts of types and degrees. Pain can be physical or emotional. Pain affects not only us but also those around us. Pain can cloud your personality and result in behavior, actions, and words that are simply not your own - they belong to the pain you are suffering. When you are hurting, you are more likely to hurt others it seems. Pain in all forms leads to seeking some sort of relief - from self-soothing, to coping mechanisms, to lashing out at others like a pressure valve blowing out.

Dogs are similar, despite their assumed ability to hide pain simply because they cannot speak; dogs reveal pain through changes in behavior like lethargy, aloofness, aggression or suddenly quick to anger. We had many dogs that came into care from other rescues or as owner surrenders due to the sudden onset of negative behavior. Jackson was a retired Sled dog who, we were told, could be dog reactive. We had him for a few days before we could get an appointment with the vet so I able to observe him with other dogs to test for myself if he was indeed aggressive or not. He was completely fine with the other Sled dogs out for our walks but did get quite upset if the others got in too close to him. I also tested him with my own pack of dogs with a similar reaction. He was completely fine if the other dogs just did

Jackson being his adorable self

their own thing but if they showed too keen an interest in him or got up in his face, he would react with snaps and growls. Dogs want to socialize through connecting with each other, it is not just through the oft noted butt sniffing that they connect but also through eye contact and nose to nose sniffing in and around the mouth and ears. Jackson found our dog Mona especially annoying because she is a "licker". As a sign of submission and/or to appease another dog, Mona will lick their face and mouth and this drove Jackson nuts! Her behavior that she used to settle a dog down was exactly the behavior that was triggering his negative reactions. We intervened to keep her away from him and once she was distracted and not trying to literally be in his face - he was fine with her. That is a cue right off the top - the fact that he was completely fine with the dogs unless they were too close told me he was truly not dog aggressive. If he was dog aggressive, he would be starting problems, he would be chasing the other dogs down, he would be attacking - but he was not doing any of that. Jackson simply did not want the other dogs around his face and head. Sure enough, once he went to the vet our suspicions were confirmed - his reactivity was tied to what could only have been extreme pain in his mouth. His teeth and gums were riddled with rot and infection from a very long time of not having any proper veterinary care. In fact, he had experienced that pain for so long, it took time for him to realize that it would not hurt anymore, even after he was fully recovered. Time and patience - and Jackson no longer experiencing that pain consistently - helped him overcome his reactivity, to relax more around the other dogs and to actually enjoy their company.

Celie is another example of pain altering one's life. Her owner surrendered Celie because she had started to snap at the family. The owner projected her own explanation for this behavior as jealousy since the woman had Celie before her husband and child so Celie obviously was being "vindictive" about having to share her owner with these two new humans. That explanation did not sit well with me. I know dogs will vie for attention and maybe get "jealous" but having that extreme of a behavior change did not make sense to me. Especially given she informed me that Celie was only acting

Celie so much happier after getting the care she needed

out in this "jealous rage" in the last six months, maybe a year. The husband had been in their lives for longer than that and so had the child. The explanation simply did not add up. I did find out that they had started keeping Celie in a crate when their child started walking. Celie was likely about seven years old at that time and was suddenly being crated for long periods of time. Celie chewed at the crate, damaging it, and she was peeing inside as well. All of these behaviors were upsetting the owner and given her thoughts on Celie's motivations - she quickly gave up her old dog for her new family. Again, once in our care and out with the pack Celie was completely fine with all the other dogs and with us - except if any got too close to her head and face. As you likely have already guessed, once we could have the vet examine her, it was clear that she was in pain. She not only had periodontal disease but chewing on the crate had torn up her mouth, even fractured a tooth! She also had a urinary tract infection - my best guess is that it was caused from being forgotten about in a crate for long periods of time. After receiving the much needed dental care and a course of medications to resolve the infection causing incontinence - Celie was a total gem. How sad that her family had just given up on her, made their own biased assumptions about her without any professional insight or assessment (please let a vet examine your dog if they suddenly start exhibiting odd behaviors - especially if you are considering surrendering or euthanizing them as your solution to the "problem"). How many people have walked away from others because they were in pain? While you cannot help others who do not want to help themselves and cannot cure a loved one's pain - give consideration to having some sympathy for their situation. Do not take their behavior or attacks personally, realize that often when someone lashes out it truly has nothing to do with you - so leave your ego and insecurities out of it. I am not saying to accept or stay if experiencing any sort of physical abuse or assault - in those cases, you must simply walk away before you get hurt further. However, if you are not in any danger or risk for your own pain - show compassion and kindness to those suffering, do not judge or antagonize them. Moreover, unlike dogs, if we are in pain - we can let others know and seek help to alleviate or reduce our pain. If we refuse to take accountability for ourselves and do not try to resolve that which is creating our pain, we are setting ourselves up to be people that we are not, to do things we would not, and say things we never would consider saying, if we were feeling well. Pain can beget more pain; misery does love company - so take care of yourself, so you can properly take care of others in your life.

It is perhaps an odd thing to say but we should also be grateful for pain. Pain is a vital part of life given that we often have to experience pain before we will change, before we will grow, before we evolve, before we get better. How often do you hear of people that only change their unhealthy lifestyle and diet after they have a heart attack or some other near death experience? Only after we hurt so bad we cannot endure any longer, do we seek out some way to alleviate the pain. Prior to running the kennel, my friend and I decided to try distance running and signed ourselves up for a local half marathon. Although we did go to a personal trainer two or three times a week, we did recognize that we would need a different style of training to accomplish distance running, so we joined a local program to properly prepare. In the weeks leading up to the race and running further and further distances in training, our bodies started to breakdown. For me it was in my hips and glutes. I started to experience pain and great stiffness. I went to a chiropractor and massage therapist regularly during the final weeks leading up to race day with the hope that once I got through the race and stopped distance running, and my body would return to normal. Well, I stopped distance running but my body never returned to the normal I had hoped for. I continued to have problems through that area seemingly regardless of my activity level. When we took over the kennel, I again hoped for great and positive changes to my body given the physical demands of the job. I walked the dogs at least 4 times a day and was often lifting and carrying dogs, food, and other supplies or equipment. I expected that because of that I would gain physical improvements of flexibility and strength while also losing weight. The exact opposite occurred during my years at the kennel I actually lost strength through my core and had limited mobility given stiffness and pain that just grew worse with every month we operated. The pain, coupled with the stress, caused me to fall into the habit of self-soothing with food which meant weight gain. Various health professionals I sought out through my time running the kennel indicated that I was actually walking too much and that I needed to do less walking and more yoga type activity. Sounded good except not feasible while working the kennel every day of the week at all hours of the day. So when we were winding down operations, I was looking forward to feeling so much better, to having time to rest and let my body heal. I was going to find that pain free normal again. It did not happen. In fact over the months immediately following the kennel closing, my pain increased and my mobility plummeted. I tried to exercise and lose weight in a variety of ways but the degradation of my body only worsened to the point that I could not stand for any amount of time without pain and I could not even sit for any amount of time without pain. One day I finally had enough - I could not take it any longer as the pain was completely interfering in my life. I went to the doctor, had x-rays done to rule out any skeletal issues and then weeks of physiotherapy and massage - treatments and exercises. My pain decreased thanks to the treatments and through the exercises, I could regain the necessary musculoskeletal strength and alignment to live my life feeling well and strong. I suffered for years before I sought out a doctor and treatment of the actual damage done, and I only made that effort, that change in my behavior, when the pain got too great to bear any longer. It was only when the pain of the status quo was greater than the pain of going to a doctor and adopting a new approach to healing and recovery did I seek that out. It is ridiculous now when I look back at those six years of suffering that I did not just take those simple steps. There were always reasons and excuses to not seek it out; not having a family doctor in the area we moved to, thinking I could just endure, that it would get better with other approaches I tried. We all do it, have done it, and will do it again in the future. It is human nature. Dogs do not seek to endure pain and discomfort, if they have the power to make that change to improve their suffering they do. They are not concerned about ego, investment of time or resources that prove to be sunk costs, or worried about hurting others feelings - if they experience pain, they will address it.

One of our dogs, Teddy, is a great example of this. After being to the vet in the afternoon for vaccinations that had been administered near his hips, he was following me out

Teddy looking confused after I woke him up from his nap

onto the deck. My aunt and uncle had come over for a visit and my uncle was coming out to the deck as well. Teddy had stopped in a section of the deck that narrowed around a corner so my uncle used his knee to push Teddy over to get past him. As he did so he also reached his hand out to pet Teddy and basically assure him he meant no harm or offense as he went by. Unfortunately, where he ended up pushing Teddy was right at the injection sight of the vaccination needle so it was very tender. The contact hurt Teddy and he snapped around to let whoever know not to touch him there, let alone push him. He was claiming his space and just indicating to stop but because my uncle was simultaneously reaching out with his hand towards Teddy's head, the snarl actually made contact and wounded my uncle. Teddy did not intend to bite anyone but he did want the pain to stop and took action to address it immediately without excuses or concerns about judgement.

Pain is pain, and always indicates something is wrong - which gives pain a tremendous value in our lives. Pain is the impetus for so many to finally make some sort of change that they have put off or ignored. We also need to be grateful for the change and the remedy that exists to ease our pain because that is not always an option. Some people do not have the option but to manage and live with their pain, we need to have empathy and compassion for those people who cannot simply solve their chronic pain. However, the norm is not for people to live in constant pain. We need to step up and take responsibility in our lives. We need to seek out remedies for the pain we are experiencing and do what we can to mitigate and prevent that pain from continuing whenever it is possible to do so.

Pain being a key driver to self-change and growth is so true. That change is so rewarding especially when you can realize relief from any pain you were experiencing. From pain, positive changes can occur - growth, evolution, innovations. So one should know that tackling that which causes discomfort can be just as powerfully rewarding. A few years ago, a book came out for women in business. Sheryl Sandberg encouraged women to "lean in". Lean in to a challenge, to pursuing dreams, and even the uncomfortable.

My work with dogs proved this is prudent advice. Leaning into a bite is the protection against it. In life one does get "bit", so to speak, more than anyone wants to. Bad things can suddenly happen; well-laid plans go awry, lied to, cheated on, accidents, disasters, illness, abandoned, injured, the list goes on and on. Sometimes you can see these bad things coming but sometimes they are totally unexpected. These situations are the "bites" in your life – they do say reality bites! In working with dogs, especially other people's dogs, and even more especially dogs that were someone else's and they gave up on them, there is apt to be the occasion that you will get bit. The dog may be aggressive but most likely scared or in pain, or maybe just not properly socialized/trained. As in life, sometimes the bites are not serious, just a nip. Sometimes the bite is more severe but you were protected in some way so the damage is minimal. Of course, sometimes the bites happen, even when you see them coming and try to avoid them, and they are nasty and painful and take a long time to heal. What I discovered is that if I leaned into the bite rather than withdraw in a panic, little to no damage was done.

It is all thanks to Barnabus that I learned this lesson. Barnabus was a wonderful, goofy old Husky who was a regular client of ours, beloved by his owners and my family. However, Barnabus was a particular fellow in that, for reasons that are not relevant to the story, he would not tolerate being touched. Not to say that you could never pet him – but, yeah, pretty much you could never really pet him! He would tolerate being physically touched but only in very short bursts and only on certain occasions ... those occasions that he would not really let you know were about to start or, more importantly, were about to end. We bonded with Barnabus out on off leash walks, he liked to dance and even play a bit. His favorite thing to do was to sing and we certainly sounded like quite the choir when we would start baying out in the orchard. He would always come when you called him and he did not negatively interact with the other dogs so there was never a desperate need to handle him, so all was well and good – usually. On the occasion of note, Barnabus was dropped off while a few other things were going on (other clients were around coming and going) so we had to keep him on his leash longer than normal. Normally we or his owner could remove the leash as soon as he was inside our gate - because the one predictable time that it was okay to handle Barnabus was in the initial few moments with him, to say hello sort of thing. By having to keep him leashed for a longer time was predictably going to be an issue. The time came that we could unclip his leash and/or his collar. My husband Jeff, bless his heart, decided that Barnabus would not bite him because he felt they had a special connection and that it was still in a reasonable amount of time to be a greeting. As I looked on, Jeff approached Barnabus, reassuring him and calm, he reached out to remove what he could and Barnabus lashed out at him with a lunge and a snap. Jeff was luckily quick enough to avoid the bite and Barnabus was not in any sort of elevated state so he did not pursue the bite. It was not at all an attack – not "I want to kill you!" It was definitely more of a correction "leave me alone buddy!" or a defense "that's my personal space sir — please respect it." So Jeff got lucky and Barnabus was not

Barnabus out exploring on a walk

overly upset because Jeff maintained his cool and was respectful of Barnabus' wishes. What I got out of the exchange was a ridiculous idea. When the exchange between Barnabus and Jeff took place, I maintained a respectful distance — so I could observe, from the side, what occurred between the two of them. From my vantage point, I was able to see and realize how to solve our issue. I thought it through, put on work gloves and chatted with Jeff about my observation and theory of how to approach our calamity. Then I calmly set about removing Barnabus' collar – via what I postulated as the fastest and lowest stressor solution. Sure enough, Barnabus tried to bite me but I knew that was pretty unavoidable in this particular circumstance. So despite the bite attempt, I did not retreat from it but just continued my calm, forward motion with that gloved hand inside the bite and with the other hand reached down to simply release his collar. Barnabus pulled away as I dropped the collar with leash attached and I withdrew as well. In all, the exchange was about 2 seconds and I was not injured despite the "bite". As for Barnabus, he was not impressed necessarily but he was not injured or at risk from a potential injury from dragging a leash around for days. We all welcomed a pleasant meander around the property together right after with our same old affection and respect for one another and me with a new understanding and insight.

Leaning in to a bite is easier said than done – it takes a calm head with a steadfast confidence in yourself. It is quite difficult to lean in to a bite because it indeed goes against our instincts, against our reflex to escape and avoid pain. You do not continue to hold onto a hot pan if it is burning you, and you most certainly do not get burned less by holding it tighter! You have to know well ahead of time - deliberately know what you will do, mentally prepare – and you have to not panic, no one thinks straight when in a panicked state. If you can do all this and manage to lean in to it – you will be surprised at the result. However, if you think about the anatomy of a dog's mouth and teeth, it makes complete sense as I had observed from my vantage point of the Barnabus and Jeff exchange. The obvious benefit to leaning into the bite is that it forces the dog's mouth further open and they lose some of the power and momentum behind the bite. In addition, if you look at the angle of a dog's teeth, you see that they have an inward curve. Dogs have evolved to bite and tear, grab a food item with their teeth and tear a piece off to chew and eat. Leaning into the bite means you are moving in the same direction of the teeth, not against it, which means less damage. Coupled with opening the jaw further, leaning in starts to make a whole lot of sense. The other aspect of leaning in to the bite that may not be visually apparent but does most definitely exist is the energy shift that occurs. Leaning into the bite gives the "bitee" the energy, the power, the control in the situation rather than the biter. In fact, for those chronic biters – those young dogs surrendered due to the owner's failure to train and guide them out of the negative puppy behavior of "nipping" – a key tactic I have used to stop this type of biting is to calmly lean in on their bites. Claiming that space and interaction to calmly redirect them onto something positive, connect with that positive element, and then reward them for desired behaviors. The dogs then learn that biting does not get them what they want – they do not gain control, attention, or the connection they seek – and they start connecting in new and positive ways.

So when life "bites" you – lean in.

Lean into the chaos, negativity, or pain as a way of positively controlling what you are able to, as a way of remaining calm and retaining your best ability to make wise decisions. Do not let the actions of others control you and your reactions – you choose how you deal with your reality. You can choose to panic. You can choose to withdraw or retreat. You can choose to cry. However, from what I have seen in my life with dogs and in my own life situations, leaning in – standing calm and resolute – to the torrent that can rip through our lives results in a much better outcome. An outcome with less damage done and with an invaluable gain of power and wisdom.

Let me begin by stating, categorically, that I am not a

psychiatrist, psychologist, mental health professional, nor do

I suffer from depression or any anxiety disorder. The

following is based on my observations of dogs and my own

life experiences. Dogs demonstrated a therapeutic approach

to some major challenges that our society is facing in this

day & age.

Leaning in to that which is not comfortable, taking on a challenge, or dealing with pain all tend to cause some level of anxiety. We can all too easily get caught up in our own heads filled with worry, self-doubts, and depression. For some reason there are so many who feel that they are not enough in some way shape or form. Perhaps it's the all the false narratives of perfection we see on one another's social media, concerns about the judgements of others, or the intense pressure we can put on ourselves to do or be more than what is humanly possible. Life can be extremely overwhelming. Life can be frightening. Life can seem like the world is out to get you. One can lose themselves into a "rabbit hole" of fear - full of worry, sadness, and isolation. When life gets like this we retreat, we want to hide from it all. We withdraw into ourselves and into our beds. However, that does not help. That withdrawal actually denies us opportunities those things that are overwhelming or scaring us. In these times, we need to take action, make meaningful connections, and work to break through that fear that has enveloped us whole. At least, this is what I have learned to do and my experiences in caring for dogs reinforced this lesson for me.

We fostered and rehabilitated hundreds of dogs for our local Humane Society who transformed into confident, well-balanced dogs simply from staying with us and sharing their time in a safe space, with a group of diverse but still balanced dogs with the simple and clear direction of merely respecting one another. The most common and yet dramatic rehabilitations are those that were fear/anxiety based. Dogs that come in to rescue have often suffered somehow –at the hand of man and/or beast – they are in a constant state of cower, no eye contact, you do not know if they even have a tail because it is tucked so far under them. These dogs are living in constant fear state with no idea of happy, only anxiety, stress, and panic. For humans, we cannot avoid the idea of "happy". All one has to do is scroll through their Facebook news feed, Twitter, Instagram, Pinterest, etc. to see some graphic or meme about happiness and living every moment like it's your last and being your best self as the meaning of life. So much is focused on always being happy, always being good – it's so "Zen" to live in the moment, but then you pressure yourself to always be good/happy/your best often simply for appearances. Dogs are not concerned about appearances or memes, they live in the moment without worrying about the future or it being their last. We seem to have this impression in our society now that everything should be good all the time, that life is not challenging and tough. Nobody is a loser, bullies are bad, adversity is to be avoided, and that we should always be happy. That is fantasy, not reality. One having the expectation to always be happy and nothing to ever go wrong creates anxiety and overwhelming pressure in itself! The reality is that one can choose to be positive/optimistic all the time but it is impossible for one to be happy all the time – it is not natural, and to medicate in order to create this unnatural state seems to remove the individual from their reality. In an attempt to find happiness without experiencing pain, discomfort, and anxiety – you actually rob yourself of those moments and times of true happiness, bliss and euphoria. Too many adults are being "fed" medications instead of being counseled on coping strategies, too many children are being "fed" medications instead of being parented on how to manage life's challenges and their emotions, too many people are being "fed" medications instead of coached on lifestyle, diet, and psychological support to lose weight, gain confidence, or overcome addiction. This is all because it requires the least amount of effort by the individual being "fed" and results in staggering, unprecedented profits for doctors and pharmaceutical companies – along with media outlets who realize advertising revenue from these same companies and significant political donations to our leaders and lawmakers.

Now I - most definitely and wholeheartedly – am not saying that there is never a need for such medications, I am saying that there seems to be an epidemic of over prescribing in our society or jumping to the prescription pad instead of dealing with reality. Our society tends to jump to address the symptoms instead of working on the root cause to overcome or prevent said symptoms. This is how our society deals with such challenges - because it is easier and because there is money to be made. This approach to mental health and behavior has carried over to our dogs.

We had clients that brought their dogs in, along with medication for their dog's anxiety. This seems to be the worst case of people projecting their issues onto their dogs. Every time we have had clients with dogs on anxiety

medication, we have asked for clarification of the need –
clarification of symptoms and dispensing – and on nearly
every occasion the medication was dispensed when the dog
was, or expected to, exhibit some sort of nuisance behavior –
barking, shaking, whining – so was on to prevent/avoid it.
Every time we would also ask if we could simply dispense if
the dogs exhibited those symptoms and not dispense if they
did not – the owners gladly accepted. This truly surprised me
to be honest, but I think it is part cost savings, part trust in
our care, and part the fact they would not be the ones to have
to "deal" with the nuisance behavior. We also asked about
the level of exercise the dogs received as well – not to make
anyone feel bad but to confirm that our care provisions could
potentially make a positive difference for the dog. We
always believed and saw proof positive of the anxiety
prevention and stress relief that exercise and socialization
make to dogs in our care. Before we took over the kennel, it
was run very traditionally – dogs in their runs for safety &
security – limited exercise and dog-to-dog interaction. There

are definite bonuses to this type of care but it was not what I felt was best for dogs entrusted to our care and that feeling was bolstered given the number of noise complaints the previous operators had had. For us to even be given a business license and allowed to operate, I had to detail how our care would be different and would prevent excess barking. Our care combined the traditional kennel care (facilities inherited on the property) with a more contemporary approach to boarding through frequent pack walks – on property, off leash – that allowed for plenty of exercise and socialization. Exercise and socialization have proven to be key components to any dog's mitigation of stress and increased enjoyment of their time here. During our years running the kennel, we did not have one noise complaint and one neighbor was even able to finally sell his home. I knew the importance of exercise – both from a human perspective and a dog's – to coping with and working through stress. There are countless reports about this correlation; I don't think I need to go into further depth in this book. However, what we noticed here – with the dogs – is the importance of exercise and socialization. Exercise alone does not seem to be the magic bullet, but socialization as part of the experience is an elixir. Where this was evident was in dogs like Rufus, Drifter, Theo, Frankie, Bailey, Hamish, Bentley, Kusko, Colby, Apollo, and the list goes on. Dogs that when first arrived were balls of fear, tension, and stress – overwhelming anxiety – on medication or not! However, with just a few walks with the pack – a group of dogs that were well balanced, respectful, and chaperoned by us humans – these dogs transformed themselves. You could tell by simply looking that their bodies were more relaxed – easy gait, fur down, ears up, tails up, mouth open, calm breathing. These dogs were able to overcome their anxiety through physical activity to allow their physiology to manage some of the stress – but also interacting with the other dogs and us, having companions that they could safely engage with – not just play, but even just lay together or walk together – made a huge difference to their ability to mitigate stress.

The reality is that anxiety happens to everyone – to overcome you must resolve to take action both physically and emotionally – the longer you wait the more the mental blocks build up, the more anxiety you get and you will end up shutdown and frozen in your fear. We witnessed the extremes of this in dogs that arguably had post-traumatic stress disorder – retired Sled dogs and what we knew as the "mountain man" dogs. Retired Sled dogs were often emotional and physical wrecks when we met them. Our society has this misconceived and romantic notion of what a Sled dog is and how they are treated. The reality that we observed time and again were dogs that were treated as commodities, not social and intelligent creatures. They are essentially warehoused, used for the monetary and notoriety gain of the human who owns them, and when they no longer are profitable, they are "discontinued" in some way. The lucky ones are retired and surrendered to find loving homes to live out their final years in warmth, love, and family. I will not detail the fate of the unlucky ones in this book. Our "mountain man" dogs were a group of dogs discovered by fortunate happenstance. Hikers doing some backwoods exploring found a couple of Border Collie "puppies" in the middle of remote wilderness. These dogs were scared and malnourished and in desperate need of care. A rescue that our local Humane Society works with regularly was called in

One of the first Mountain Man pups to arrive into care, cute but scared

by local law enforcement once it was discovered where these dogs had come from, the conditions they were kept in, and the number of other dogs that were present and also in need of care. These dogs had never seen a veterinarian and were living off vats of discarded restaurant fryer grease and garbage. They had had little to no contact with human beings or other dogs. Retired Sled dogs at least know other dogs are dogs and people are people - these "mountain man" dogs had no idea that they were dogs and were paralyzed with fear around other, even calm, dogs. The commonality of these dogs that came into our care was that they had lived away from civilization and unprotected outdoors. Dogs that have lived their lives outside become incredibly attune to their surroundings and any changes in it. This sensitivity serves them well for survival purposes while living outdoors but completely overwhelms them when initially introduced to our environments filled with noise, vehicles, traffic, other creatures, and other strange objects (Trixie, a retired Sled dog, was terrified of ceiling fans) all around. The dogs need to learn how to cope in these new environments to fully explore and enjoy all that they have to offer. They learn that a walk along the ocean is a joyful and fun experience even if terrified when they first see and hear the beach. If these dogs

Trixie was one of the more confident Sled dogs but ceiling fans terrified her

were allowed to simply exist in their comfort zone - huddled in a corner - avoiding the world, they never overcame their stressed state. However, when the dogs could connect with another dog - a balanced dog – they could learn to trust both that dog and us. They could start to overcome their fears and stress. They would start by simply following us out on walks around the yard. A relatively safe, controlled space where most of the outside world was kept at bay beyond the fences. The simple following would morph into baby steps of confidence and new comforts, the surprise nuzzles and licks of your hand from behind, the sudden interest in playing with that dog they find comfort with, even them finally being comfortable making eye contact with you or coming in for love and attention from the front of you. Yes, they were that scared initially - eye contact or front facing encounters were pure terror for them. However, if kept safe and positively rewarded for those little steps, they could start to build up a confidence and resilience that led to new discoveries of joy in new places, with other people, and other dogs. The key was always found in simply taking those seemingly small steps and really appreciating and recognizing the importance of those little efforts that over time make up the foundation for overcoming fear, conquering anxieties, and coping with stress. We would honestly not even realize the progress we were making in the days of working with the dogs - it was only in those more intermittent encounters of having volunteers coming and interacting with dogs that we would get the feedback of how different the dogs were, how they were so much less stressed, and so much happier.

Further evidence was proven in those dogs that only get the exercise but cannot safely socialize due to their issues with aggression or dog reactivity. Brewser was a dog that could not exercise with the other dogs because he was dog reactive. I would spend hours with him in the day – walking, playing, and even just sitting with him when he was tired out simply because of his anxiety when he was in his enclosure. The second to last day of his stay, I had to call out to a dog while I was outside the kennel building that Brewser was housed in. I immediately heard a disturbance of considerable size as Brewser expressed his anxiety in a very physical way. We rushed to put all the other dogs in to check on what was going on with Brewser. To our surprise, when we opened the door to the building Brewser was standing there after forcing his way out of his chain link enclosure. The metal fencing was ripped up and away from the frame and his muzzle was beaten up from the effort. We had to move him into the office (drywall can be scratched and destroyed without the dog being injured) and continued to spend an enormous amount of time with him for his last day prior to checking out because he so desperately needed that socialization element – so desperate that he injured himself. Brewser served as proof that exercise alone does not fully address stress and anxiety. He was the puzzle of a dog that we could not solve. His stays with us did not help him, he did not have a breakthrough, he did not work through his stress and anxiety. He was the only dog that had anxiety & stress that we could only exercise and not dog socialize. Brewser served as further evidence of the need to not only exercise, but also socialize with others, to successfully overcome your anxiety and stress.

Social media has allowed us to share ourselves with the world but typically in very shallow ways. Those facades and filters make it easy for us to simply and literally keep up appearances. Our connections siphoned through technology skew reality of those connections and the details of our lives. When that is all we see of other's lives - the picture perfectness, we feel both shame for our flaws and pressure to be perfect. We fixate on how we look to others and are all too quick to judge those that we worry are judging us. We are too concerned about what other people see, what they think. Much like focusing too much on language and not intent - we neglect to be concerned about feelings, emotions, and truths. We are too quick to think negatively, to judge, to blame, without any real concern about the impact of those thoughts, judgments, and blame. When we go to visit family and friends, there is too much concern for cleanliness over connection. When we are out and about and we see people struggling, we are quick to pass judgment and slow to offer any understanding or help. When we walk into a room of strangers, we are more focused on what those strangers are thinking about us than the occasion that has brought us all together. The best example of this harmful preoccupation in dogs is when a dog is too fixated on what they see. Dogs who are obsessed to the point of manic about what they can see. Constantly looking off in the distance and all around seemingly looking for something, anything to react to. The most balanced dogs use more than just their eyes to explore their world, especially when you consider the incredible dynamics of their sense of smell. A dog's sense of smell is well known to be far more powerful than a human being's. Given the physiological importance of the dog's olfactory system, it is only logical that they have a critical need to use it. A dog needs to engage its nose to fully explore its environment and to work its brain out. Working a dog's sense of smell on a walk, works out their brains as well as their bodies. The result of which is a dog that is best able to work through anxieties, stress, frustrations, and excitement. So often, we saw dogs in need of behavior rehabilitation that were denied the ability to use their nose to explore their world. They were tied up, severely limiting their exploration of their world across all their senses but there were those dogs that were exhibiting problematic behaviors who were walked every day, multiple walks a day. Their owners had done what they had been told to. They were walking their dogs and walking them multiple times a day and for sometimes over an hour at a time. Yet still had ongoing and ever challenging issues with their dog's behavior. Well, as one dog trainer once told me - not all walks are created equal. Yes, walks are vitally important to the health and welfare of any dog but limiting the dogs walk to just walking without the ability to fully experience their environment seemed to frustrate some of these dogs. These dogs would act out, never settle, easily trigger to reactions that could be aggressive. All too often, these dogs were large and, I hate to say it, owned or at least most often walked by people who could not physically handle such big, strong dogs. These owners were trying their best but needed to use various "tools" in order to manage their dog through controlling their head or neck. These "tools" tended to severely inhibit the dogs experience on a walk, resulting in bad behaviors and occasionally bad relations with their owners. The walks these dogs were getting were not draining their energy, in fact the stress and frustration that seemed to result from such walks only served to compound negative energy. To be healthy, dogs needs to experience life beyond what they can see. When these dogs came into our care what seemed to be the best therapy was simply allowing them the opportunity to run, to play, to chase, to explore unencumbered for at least a few days. One dog in particular stands out in my memory, a female Yellow Lab mix, Kimmy. Kimmy had been adopted from another rescue before her family moved to our area.

Kimmy having some fun mud bogging during our pack walk

They had had Kimmy for a couple years before bringing her to me to see if she was a candidate for the behavior rehabilitation we could offer. They said she had struggled with a bit of anxiety since they had first brought her home. Her mom was doing all she could to try to help her overcome this but with no success. They actually worried that Kimmy was getting worse than better. She did not seem just anxious any more, she was getting more and more reactive. I had them leave Kimmy with me for a night or two so I could assess her behavior to know if we could help. What I experienced was a wonderful dog! A dog that seemed exhale and just relax with us. She was not reactive to the other dogs. I could tell she was tightly wound for some reason but she was really embracing the care we could provide. Her short stay was like a little doggy therapy for her so I knew we could make a difference for this dog. Her parents booked her in for a rehabilitation stay and I kept them updated to the progress we made during her weeks with us. I will admit that I was a bit confused about the behaviors they shared with me they were experiencing with Kimmy. The reported anxiety, reactivity, and aggression never occurred with us. I asked for more details and found out that Kimmy's mom, who was the one who typically walk her, was using a "tool" that gave her control over Kimmy's head. She had found this was the only way she could control Kimmy. The problem is this piece of equipment, by giving the handler completely control of the dogs head, robs the dog of any opportunity to engage its nose. The dog walker can keep the dogs head up and behind the walkers body most easily. This is wonderful control for the handler and is wonderful for the old school definition of a "heel" when walking a dog. However, micromanaging a dogs body to this degree when out for walks in various environments only serves to excessively, and arguably dangerously, engage the dogs use of their eyes to interact with their world, to experience their surroundings, and any triggers that may be in it. Kimmy lost all her anxiety when she was with us. You could physically see her body was more relaxed and her behavior was a wonderful balance of play and calm. She felt confident and trusted both, me and our pack of dogs. To show the potential that Kimmy had, I took her to our local downtown for an on leash walk. On my walk though I chose a chest clasp style harness. This style of harness allowed me to control Kimmy if she surprisingly lunged or reacted to anything while still giving Kimmy control over her own head and empowered her to explore through her nose as well as her eyes. Kimmy did wonderfully and showed no signs of stress or negative reaction. The walk served as good exercise and experience, and a great example of what her mom could do to continue to best support Kimmy's physical and mental wellbeing.

This type of story was repeated time and again in both dogs surrendered to the rescue as well as clients dogs brought in for behavior rehabilitation. Each dog suffered from being exclusively allowed to use their eyes to explore their world and this often created the state of them "existing too much in their head". They were easily triggered by any sort of visual cue and were quick to react negatively - they did not fully sense their world and that seemed to lead to unhealthy behavior. If one is only concerned about what is seen or how we appear to others, we lose touch - literally and figuratively - to what life can be and should be. By only being concerned by the surface, about looks, about material "things", about labels, about Instagram photos, and viral videos - we are not living in a truly healthy and balanced way. Life is so much more than looks, we need to worry less about what people think, about what they see, and more about someone's experience with us - how did we make them feel, how did we enrich their lives, what have we done to make them happy, help them heal, or share a laugh? Our lives would be vastly improved if we committed more to fully experiencing it rather than simply worrying if we "look" good. We need avoid falling into unconscious consumerism, idolizing money, of never having or being enough, we are a society that readily justifies and encourages greed and gluttony. We need to embrace the true idea that we are more, we are better if we seek less, give more, and reduce our negative impact on our bodies, other people, and our planet. We need to commit to looking beyond appearances. We need to appreciate those with whom we share a connection for who they are beyond how they look, the clothes they wear, and how shiny their floor is. We would all be less anxious and judgmental if we can focus less on what we see on the outside and on nurturing what we know is on the inside.

As a society, we need to prescribe less and converse and exercise more. We need more than just Facebook friends & Twitter followers – we need true friends to hug, to have shoulders to cry on and to share actual experiences with. We need to visit the pharmacy less and the park more. We need to post less and do more. We need to look into another person's eyes instead of staring at a computer screen or our smartphones. We have lost ourselves in our pursuit of happiness, pursuit of profits, and pursuit of all things greener – all a siren's song! Behind the facades of social media and the clickbait headlines are real people. Real people who need to connect to each other in a real way – a true and honest way

– for us all to heal and move through our stresses, our anxieties, and our pains. To experience true happiness, true love, and true passion one must live in truth; and truth can be tough to hear, to bear and to live with. However, in that truth, in that reality you will find love and happiness that make it worth it all. If in doubt, just look in the eyes of a dog, you will see a truth and authenticity that speak to your soul.

Sheep in Wolf's Clothing

So much of what we experience stress and anxiety over is tied to our perception of ourselves. Human beings can often be sabotaged by our ego versus our insecurities. We are overwhelmed with messaging - advertisements, media, and entertainment - that directly and indirectly pushes societal ideals upon us. That happy and successful people are typically white, thin, straight, wealthy, and young - perhaps, they even use a particular product or service or live a certain lifestyle. If you buy in, you will be happy and successful - and if you are still not happy then must be because you are not the other factors. If you were white, thin, straight, wealthy, and young you would be happy with the product. Or even more hideously, maybe the suggestion is that if you purchase, you will become white, thin, straight, wealthy, and young - or as near as possible to that ideal. That is how one is happy, right? The magical potion for happiness - if you are those ideals, you will be happy, you will be successful, you will be fulfilled. The odd thing is, that is not true. How many white, thin, straight, wealthy, and young people in the world are depressed? Live in pain? Feel unloved?

Another truth is that there are happy people out there that have none of those "ideal" traits. That is not to say that there is anyone in this world that does not have struggles and challenges to overcome. Rather, it is despite our struggles and challenges people can choose to have a positive attitude, to be happy. What I have experienced in my life taught me this lesson years ago. I was fortunate enough to be part of a Development Tour to Africa in the summer before I began grade 12. The United Nations, Save the Children Fund, and the Canadian government sponsored our group, thus allowing us greater access and immersion into the local culture and communities than regular tourists. We were able to visit various projects that not only our sponsors were a part of but also local NGOs (Non-Governmental Organizations). We spent time with African families both in the city and in remote villages. One of our first stops on our six-week trip was the village of Vuti in Zimbabwe. We tented in amongst the huts of the villagers for a night or two and were able to spend time with various families in the village, visit the local school, and work with the women in the fields and retrieving water. A genuine attempt for us to all understand the lives the villagers lived. Our visit of course was not their usual day, they were excited to share their lives with us and celebrated us being there through songs and dance around a fire our first night. We all sang, clapped, and danced for hours - it was a phenomenal experience, a true gift. A gift not just of being with these people but seeing the genuine joy that completely embodied these individuals. These individuals who have relatively little in regards to material wealth, who do not have indoor plumbing, who have to haul water, who work every moment of their day to just survive really. They are working on food gathering and preparation, working on gathering cotton to sell or make textiles from, working on keeping home and clothes clean, raising children, etc. - from dawn until dusk, always working, always living. That night around the fire though, there was no mention of work, no complaining about the conditions in which they live, no exhaustion at all, there was simply elation and revelry. All just beamed with happiness and joy to have us with them and for them to be together. The best dancers performed, and the drummers were amazing. The villagers loved not just performing but also taking the care and time to teach each of us how to sing, drum, or dance along with them. They let us into their community and their hearts with genuine love and happiness. It was very moving to watch the grandmother that I was closest to clapping along with so much enthusiasm and contentment I had rarely seen in anyone. She even explained that how she was clapping - with right hand on top of left - indicated she was happy (that is what she told me, but I don't know if that is a universal truth at all). Despite the challenges they faced in their lives, they were happy. Without all the material trappings of our society, these people embraced joy and celebrated us being there. It and they were amazing! More recently in life, it was again dogs that reinforced this lesson for me. I think this is an aspect of dogs that endears them to us. They are often happy - and they show us they are happy. They are happy to see us - even if we just left the room for a few minutes. They are happy to go out in the yard, happy to go for a walk, happy to play, happy to snuggle. They show they are happy too - their tails wag, their bodies are relaxed or wiggling back and forth with their tails, eyes softened but engaged - they may even jump up, lick, or bark. What makes them so happy? Well as much as maybe a toy or a treat can in the moment - what makes a dog happy is attention and affection from their humans and other dogs. A dog's joy - needs no toys - it is rooted in relationships. It is engaging and interacting with others that make dogs happy and content. It brings them joy to connect with others - they are social animals and socialization is key to their emotional welfare.

They are just like us. If we retreat into ourselves, as we become "global" on the World Wide Web but lose sense of family and community, we lose our natural abilities to cope with life and isolate ourselves from true sources of long-term joy. When we lean on medications rather than a support system, we can find ourselves not only numb to pain and anxieties but also to happiness and excitement. These medications can be so vile when they practically make us emotional zombies. It is a sad thing to witness, but that sadness is only compounded when one realizes that there are so many thousands out there that had other choices available to help them. Other choices that involve exercise and socialization are more difficult to do rather than just swallowing a pill, but as with so many things in life - often those things that are most worth doing are not the easiest things to do. Again, sometimes you have to take responsibility for yourself, even - or especially - when it comes to your health and welfare. There are more aspects to our lives than a doctor can fix for us. It is time to take care of ourselves better emotionally, mentally, and physically.

Anxiety in our being can create insecurity, which then creates more anxiety. Insecurity is an insidious creature. It seems so easy to be insecure about yourself. That confidence without arrogance is such a delicate balance of love, experience, modesty, and social aptitude. Insecurity is something that affects all of us in our lives, something that occurs as a factor of our youth and personality. As you grow up, you are faced with your entire existence being learning; learning how to walk, talk, read, live. Self-assuredness is built over time with love and support from those that you can trust to not judge; to critique not criticize, those that will encourage you to keep trying, those that will pick you up instead of step on you in the process of learning and growing. Arguably, insecurity should not even exist any longer - in this day and age of understanding of psychology, of communication, of sharing, of technology, anything that people could be insecure about can be healed. Enough enlightenment exists in this world to overcome our insecurities. Yes, I suppose so - logically, rationally - yes that is true. However, insecurity is not rational. It is a fear in that way. Compounded by the fact that many insecurities are not a true representation of reality but rather one's perception and experiences that have skewed their beliefs in and about themselves. Insecurity does not only affect the individual though. Insecurity is insidious and snakes its way into your interactions and relationships. I prefer to know where I stand with someone so that is where my opinion of insecurity as being insidious comes from. Insecure folks will not have the conviction to be honest to your face. They will be kind or diminutive while you are present but once you are gone, they lash out and will spread negative opinions, stories, and even facts about you to feel better about themselves. They are a nasty people and the noxious bit is that because their vileness is based in insecurity they will often position themselves as the victim. The term passive-aggressive is common for a reason. It is all too common because insecurity seems to permeate through society with no regard for age, gender, race, economics, or geography. It is especially troublesome as the typical victims of insecure bullies are the weakest in the group. These victims - the meek and the powerless - are those whose experiences end in the most devastating ways, like suicide and shootings. It is heartbreaking in so many ways. Insecurity is a nasty saboteur of relationships in couples, families, and among friends as well as in a dog pack. We occasionally would have a dog come in to our care that was just a bit "off", it may take a walk or two for us to confirm the dog's issues but the other dogs would typically pick up on the idiosyncrasy quite quickly. The best example of this is Howlett. Howlett came in from another rescue, which was very common for us since our location afforded many more potential adopters than more remote organizations. Howlett was adorable looking but he did have a certain degree of dissonance in his gaze. We interacted with him on his own initially - standard assessment practice to get a sense of the dog and any issues they may have to overcome. Once I was able to get a better read on Howlett and his behavior and energy level, I introduced him to my family pack of dogs, all of whom are extremely dog savvy - all confident and non-reactive. They all walked well together and engaged in play with Howlett without issue. So despite some initial reservations that something just off, that all was not as it seemed with him, over the course of the next few days we introduced him to the pack and all was well. I questioned my reservations and initial assessment as more and more walks went on without incident or concern. It was about two weeks into his stay with us that it all started to change and those initial concerns were validated. On our afternoon walk all was going as usual, the pack was only about 7 dogs so nothing too overwhelming or concerning. At the time of this walk, we were in just our oversized backyard with its fountain, large garden area and numerous hedges. On property at the time, we had a group of movie dogs and their trainers staying with us. A couple of the trainers were nearby having lunch and we started to chat over the fence about whatever trivial thing we chatted about. Suddenly, there was chaos in the pack and Howlett was attempting to attack a very submissive female who usually just played with her sister dog apart from the rest of the pack. Howlett had jumped on her and was chasing her when I turned. I ran to rescue the female as he launched himself onto her in an attempt to latch onto her back. I grabbed his collar and held him back from the other dogs while my team calmed the pack and the trainers having lunch retrieved a leash I had hanging on the fence and helped me leave the yard with Howlett while having the pack not follow us. After that occurrence, I became concerned about how and if Howlett could be trusted. After days of walking him on his own, I re-introduced him to our family dog Mona. Mona has excellent dog sense - I implicitly trust her instincts and understanding of other dogs. So I had her come with me to walk Howlett off leash around the property. As they ran around playing and having fun, there was no incident and zero concerns were raised of any issue or repeat attack. I know Mona is not a true submissive but she also is not dominant - she knows when to be strong and when to back away. So I just watched them but more importantly, once I knew Howlett was not going to attack her, I watched Mona. After a few minutes of observation, I had the realization that Mona indeed knew exactly how to interact with Howlett. Despite them running around in every direction, Mona never allowed Howlett to get behind her. She always kept him in front of her while they were playing. When they did play chase, she never allowed herself to be the prey in their chase game. Mona knew to manage Howlett simply by never turning her back to him. I began introducing Howlett back to a pack of dogs but I handpicked the group with whom he would engage. He could only walk with confident dogs that all seemed to be attuned to keeping him within sight and all had a fantastic time with him. We had a few people apply to adopt Howlett at this time but I just knew he was not ready to be adopted without it being a potential disaster. In an attempt to expedite his rehabilitation, the rescue group chose to place him in a private foster home, with no other dogs, where he could be simply socialized on occasion to build up over time. It was only a short time later that I received a copy of a video that the foster family had taken questioning my assessment of Howlett as potentially an unpredictable danger. The video was about two minutes long and showed Howlett playing with another dog that belonged to the foster family's friends. While the foster family did not lambaste me in their note to the Humane Society, they did completely contradict my assessment to use caution around other dogs with Howlett - using the video as proof. However, what the family neglected to see in the video was that, much like Mona, the second dog in the video never once turned its back to Howlett. I shared my observation about the video and noted it was perhaps too soon for Howlett to feel emboldened enough to get aggressive with the other dog. I heard no other progress reports or assessments over the next week or two. Then I got the call that there had been an issue with another dog - nothing serious but enough for the fosters to feel out of their comfort zone. Howlett was coming back to me for continued fostering and rehabilitation. All finally agreed it was going to take a long time for him to overcome his social issues. He was with me for a week or two more.

He ran with those same big, strong, and confident Humane Society dogs as before. The only incident occurring when a bird in some bushes suddenly distracted another dog and since Howlett was well ahead of him, the dog turned and headed into the bush to investigate. I witnessed his diversion and immediately checked where Howlett was. Howlett had unfortunately heard the rustle in the bushes as well and his casual glance back was suddenly an intense double take as he turned and raced to the dog and launched himself onto that dog's back and tried to latch on to the back of his neck. Luckily, not only was I there within seconds because I had been only a few feet away but the dog Howlett had jumped on was a large Husky cross that was well protected by his dense mane of fur. Howlett had only grabbed at fur as I pulled him off and separated the two dogs. No harm but most definite a foul that the other dogs in that pack would not easily overcome with Howlett in their group. Fortunately, another foster who could also do long-term rehabilitation at his property and with his dogs was soon able to take Howlett on. He worked with Howlett for months and months, Howlett regained his confidence and calm. This new and improved dog could now be safely adopted to a very supportive and loving home. His rehabilitation took a lot of time and required the work of a few people and many fantastic dogs that could help balance him out and teach him healthy social behavior. His insecurity had made him dangerous, had made him unpredictable, and had made him disruptive to the peace of any pack.

This is what insecurity does to people too. Those that are insecure are hard to predict because that insecurity is exactly why they will not attack but also why they will. The insecure may initially doubt themselves. They need time to build up their courage and to size up the others in the group. That is why those riddled with insecurity do not come right out with their judgments and bullying. They are building up their courage and assessing the group they are in first and then will attack the weak when they are not prepared nor aware of the attack happening. The truth is that we all have elements of insecurity within us that we have to choose to not listen to. We have to rise up against the doubts and nastiness in our psyches and have a voice at the table of who we are. Insecurities are difficult to overcome - in fact, I would argue that we never completely get over them - but in the end, you have to choose to understand and accept yourself for who you are. Make yourself your biggest concern and not be overly concerned about others. You do not need to compare yourself to them and you do not need to fall victim to their judgments of you. Losing your insecurity not only benefits you but also those around you.

Insecurity can cause one to adopt an irrational need for control. Control seems to be what so many strive for nowadays. We have seemed to increase the intensity of our lives and truly relaxed our commitment of time to family, friends, and community less. It feels like more than ever people are struggling for control in their lives and one can only speculate there are a few driving factors for this. Personally, when I have been truly worried about control is when I lacked faith and trust in others. In those situations, I believed those others would not do something good enough or worse - that their actions would actually cause harm. By harm, I do mean in a variety of ways from harming the efforts towards achieving a goal for an organization, all the way to actually physically harming me. I felt the need to be in control of those situations. There is also the flip side to this strong desire for control, that when I have not held that control I have been harmed. This lack of control is defeating and causes not only depression, but also desperation. In the most serious situation, in that extreme, we can see that the cause of one's need to control is rooted in a lack of security. Those who lack security - not just physically - are those that seek out control in order to protect themselves and/or to improve their position in some way. That obsessive and unhealthy fixation on control is rooted not in confidence or expertise but rather in fear. A controlling personality is often erratic and unsettled. They do not make good leaders, as they do not inspire confidence or loyalty. One desperate for control typically is seen as a tyrant to some degree as they attempt to force their will on others. If they succeed in this hostile takeover of the relationship or situation, they are resented for their tactics and if unsuccessful, there will still be a negative reaction to the attempt and the need to defend against it. As with all things, there is of course a balance that is healthy, a measured need for control in which you control yourself - your actions and your emotions - but do not feel the need to impose your will onto others. That

Drifter giving me a wink after we figured him out

balance is where you will find confidence and stability.

As with humans, you do see some dogs with an unhealthy need to control others or their environment. This determination for control will typically manifest in excessive physicality or excessive vocalization. The physicality can be dangerous. There are a few examples that I have witnessed in the years of working with dogs. The first, Drifter, was one of a few large dogs that were very aware of their size and were very insecure and nervous. His owners had advised that he seemed overly protective - even reactive - despite his overall nervous tendencies and fears that they had seen him demonstrate. They chose to have us care for him while they were away because we could offer supervised socialization that we all hoped would help improve his confidence and help to calm him. He avoided contact with the other dogs initially. Drifter acted completely indifferent which was not problematic as he would still exercise and follow the pack but did not engage in any interactions with the other dogs. This avoidance lasted for a few days and then I noticed Drifter was starting to walk more amongst the pack. I was happy initially because at first glance I took his actions to mean he was coming out of his shell and our efforts to help his behavior were working. However, what I was observing had an odd energy and intention about it - it felt different, not friendly or curious, but rather full of tension. Drifter was approaching each dog, sidling up to each in what seemed to be basically a sizing up. My assessment proved true - as Drifter was indeed sizing himself up against the others as well as building up his courage to take control of the pack. After one or two walks with this behavior, Drifter made his move and launched an attack at whom he had pegged as a beatable. He angled to come from behind the German Shepherd he was targeting and pinned him down. We were there in mere seconds and I was beyond grateful that the two of us are quite strong as it took us both to safely remove Drifter from not just the fracas but also the ensuing eruption of chaos as the pack rallied against the erratic and unwarranted aggression. Thankfully all settled quickly and without any injury to dog or person but we knew that Drifter could not socialize with the group as a whole. We could not trust him to not attack another - he was a bully. He was masking his own fears and anxieties through lashing out at others. Targeting his attacks on dogs that he could overpower. We had to keep the other dogs safe but we also needed to care for Drifter in a healthy way. We did not want to deny him of that critical socialization though so we simply selected those dogs that we knew were soft enough to not trigger him - quiet, older females. Drifter did wonderfully for the rest of his stay - the select socialization did actually improve his overall mental state, as he was more relaxed and even playful. The key was for him to feel in control of his space and if that was not possible (which it often is not) then he needed to be in a space in which he held no fear, a space without any perceived threats, that was a space that he could just exist without having to be in control of it. He could let go of feeling as if he needed to bully others and it made him and those around him, happier and healthier. Bullies are lacking in some way and that manifests into aggression and cruel behaviors to control and negatively others and their environment. Bullies cannot be allowed to harm others but they also will only be further damaged if they are demonized and attacked. Of course, this is all within reason and only applicable to those bullies that can be helped. Those that can open themselves up to others to connect, reveal their vulnerabilities and share their needs in order to overcome that which they lack. Once they can fill those voids in themselves and heal, they will be able change their ways and let go of their need for control.

Another example of control through physicality is at the other end of the spectrum of size and a small Chihuahua cross that came into the rescue, surrendered by its owner for aggression. Little Shermie had apparently nipped his owners hand so they surrendered him to the Humane Society. To be clear, there is a difference between a bite and a nip and mouthing. What Shermie had done was nipped at the owner's hand - did not break skin, just more snapped back at, growled and snarled and generally looked vicious. This was very atypical behavior and shocked them so they felt they could not trust him any longer. Shermie was a complete love of a

An attentive Shermie, he just wanted some respect

dog for us - great and loving with people and very good with the other dogs. We were honestly quite confused as to the how on earth he had been triggered to such a violent reaction. We went for over a week without any issues, just were truly saddened that this rock solid dog was surrendered simply for a one-time mistake. When we finally saw a flash of aggression from Shermie was when we were out for a walk with the small dogs and it suddenly starting to downpour. We called for all the dogs and all but Shermie made their way in. While the other walker secured the group of dogs who had run in, I headed back out to connect with Shermie. He had hidden in the gazebo and was not wanting to come when I called him. So I jogged out to where he stood and just went to scoop him up to carry him in. That is what set him off and was his trigger to react with aggression. He surprised me a bit but I immediately knew what the issue was. I slowed myself down, calmed us both, and then allowed him to come to me. He settled and happily approached me, I put him on a leash rather than pick him up and we headed in. It was the lack of control, Shermie was reacting to. Shermie was the first little dog that showed us this behavior but most certainly not the last. It is all too common for people to take away a small dogs power, to simply force their will upon the small dog because they can. Owners will often treat their small dog much differently than they would a big dog - a great example is exactly the exchange Shermie and I had, rather than calling a small dog and allowing it the time to make that decision to comply, owners will just go pick the dog up - something impossible with a large breed dog. Acts such as these rob a small dog of its power and autonomy to be a dog, a creature that has a mind and will of its own. By consistently undermining the dog being a dog, you will see the dog either develop anxiety and/or aggression. That is their only option when they are not allowed to make choices and behave how they wish, if they are constantly just forced to do things and go places without even being given the option it will just chip away at their sense of self. It erodes their confidence and causes them to have to lash out in order to achieve some control over their bodies. If they are never given the opportunity to be who they are, if they are never given a chance to make their own decisions to follow your lead (or not) - you stress that dog terribly and that resulting aggression is not the dog's fault but rather a factor of your overhandling and disrespect of it. Sometimes how people choose to "love" their dog is not what is actually best for the dog's well-being. Taking away a living, breathing, sentient being's autonomy, removes its sense of security, which can trigger a desperate reaction - aggression - to achieve some sort of control over its body and environment. The creature feels no other alternative besides aggression to claim the space in which it exists because its cues and body language have been ignored. The need to control through lashing out can be a sudden onset change in behavior. This is typically a result of individuals who have been overpowered, imposed upon, or exploited. The meek can be forced into being dangerous if they lack that security and control over themselves. When you feel completely powerless given how someone is mistreating you and robbing you of any control you have over your life, you think only extreme measures can save you. After surviving my abusive relationship, I went for counselling. I knew I needed help to understand my part in those relationships that had harmed me not just physically but also psychologically. I struggled with trust - both in others and myself, but also had a level of guilt. I blamed myself for being in the relationship as well as for horrible thoughts I had feeling those were my only means of escape. I had wished for my ex-boyfriend, my abuser, to go to prison or even to be killed in some altercation that he started - since he seemed to have a predisposition for violence. In my youth, growing up in a home with a not so kind stepfather I had even considered poisoning his tea somehow. It seemed that as long as these men existed in my world I was not safe and never would be. I was completely and utterly powerless to protect myself so the only option that assured my security was for them to not exist. It is beyond extreme and I bore a great amount of guilt for even thinking such things. However, what the counselor shared with me is that such thoughts are very common and completely natural for people in similar situations. If it seems like you have no other option, if you have tried everything to protect yourself or change the abuser, you consider the extreme as your only means of escaping their control.

Another type of control attempt is through noise. The one who talks loudest is heard, the squeaky wheel gets the grease. When you start to lose control of a situation or your emotions you may find yourself talking louder or even shouting. If someone is yelling at you, you may very well yell back, even louder. If you are trying to be in control of your environment, you seek out silence - like when needing to focus on work or at least only that noise that you want to pay attention to - like watching a movie. Noise can be as imposing as a physical entity. Actually, given the fact that noise cannot be as easily blocked as a physical presence, noise is more obtrusive than the physical. It is difficult to protect yourself from noise and noise can definitely be used to control. It is another form of energy - physical force is one thing but noise is energy too. Noise is a very common means to control one's environment and other people. In our lives noises are used for positive and negative control - look at the use of sirens by first responders or fire alarms as positive ways to control behavior through noise, a negative way would be yelling at loved ones. Dogs use noises in order to communicate in all sorts of ways - barking, growling, whining. However, dogs have language beyond vocalizations - relying heavily on body language and energy to communicate with us and each other.

Often they will experience frustration of sorts simply because people do not understand the dog's signals and messages. All too many people are completely illiterate in understanding their dog's body language and energy cues. It is a personal pet peeve (pun intended) to see some of these viral videos that circulate as "so cute" with a young child hanging off of a dog that is clearly not comfortable, is scared, or anxious. It is not cute - especially when dogs lose their lives due to human ignorance. Those instances where a pet owner ignores or does not know how to recognize the stress that their dog is experiencing that results in the dog biting or attacking then lose its life branded as "dangerous".

Thankfully, there are times that people who do not understand their dogs simply get so frustrated with the situation that they surrender them rather than waiting until the worst happens. When I first met Mona, she was a complete bundle of pent up energy. She drove me completely bonkers. She was about 2 years old, intact, and was in dire need of regular exercise and socialization. Mona

A sure way to keep Mona quiet - put a toy in her mouth!

had lived with a family with many kids. With so much going on in that home, Mona was not a top priority. Mona was desperate for a say in her life and by that I mean literally. She was bursting with erratic energy from seemingly raging hormones and restricted activity. She was extremely needy of any attention she could get. I speculated from her behavior that Mona had had little to no control in her life growing up. In a home with so much going on, the dog was likely an afterthought, a chore or an inconvenience. However, we now had a dog that had learned she could get what she wanted - get attention, get outside, get fed - by being the loudest creature in the area. When I would walk by her with my focus on something or someone else, Mona had a special skill of jumping up to deliver a piercing, sharp bark directly into my ear. It is no exaggeration that I had to double check that my ear canal was not bleeding on a regular basis. Whenever she was not getting exactly her way, she would bark and bark and bark. She had learned while growing up that she got her way when she barked and that barking helped to vent some of her energy. I found it annoying at first but once I figured out what her motivations seemed to be, why she was barking so much - she wanted control - I could then work to help her overcome. That help came through having her spayed and having her exercise and socialize at least 4 times a day. She was initially adopted quite quickly but brought back because of her vocalizations. If she was not barking, she was whining. The constant noise was not endearing Mona to anyone. In fact the adopters did not believe that she was at all more settled than when she first had come into care. They simply found her constant whining and barking unbearable. They simply could not stand to live with her. Once she was back with us, I could focus on really helping her overcome the anxiousness that she had. We focused on making sure that she was well exercised of course, but we went further. We tried to provide for her needs before she realized she needed it. We also ignored - despite the ear pain - her barking when we were certain she was completely fine. It took time, she was in care for months and she improved leaps and bounds. As her confidence grew, her anxiousness waned. She walked more and barked less, she played more and whined less. Mona could still slip into the old behaviors but she was so much more settled, calm, and confident - she was becoming a balanced and loving dog who actually was remarkably intuitive with other dogs. In the end, the lucky family that adopted Mona was our own. In the few months leading up to this adoption, we had lost two of our dogs. We had just decided to adopt a wonderful young male dog that was in high demand to be adopted with many applications for him. It was out of guilt for keeping the "easy" dog, I felt that we should take the "hard" dog too. The family agreed, we saw Mona as a challenge but she had also proven to be a fantastic dog with other dogs. She helped me do the work of saving dogs' lives through healthy rehabilitation. Now years later, Mona will still bark when things are not under her control - like when her two brothers play fight and she wants them to stop or to allow her to join in. She still whines, sometimes for no apparent reason other than to get the attention of one of us or one of the other pets. So she still can default into those behaviors that she grew up needing, but for the most part she has grown and developed beyond the need to control everything to assure her that she is cared for. She knows she is loved, she is safe, and she will be for her whole life. She is doing good and she knows it. She also knows she has to be quiet when she is sneaking around eating the cat's food. ;-)

Dogs showed me that it is not healthy and balanced individuals that seek to control everything and everyone around them. Those who have an irrational need for control are motivated by some sort of negative experience they have had in their life. These "control freaks" have anxiety issues in some degree and no longer trust things to be okay for them. Their past has shown them that in order for them to be cared for and their security assured, that it could not be left to others to do. They have been let down in serious ways, so serious that it has completely dominated their behavior in every moment of their lives. Next time you encounter someone who always needs control - try to not react with anger, try not to be offended - but rather try to be understanding and allow some consideration to why they insist on control. Being compassionate and compliant, as long as their being in control does no harm to you or others, can help everyone move forward. By allowing that person the control they so desperately seem to need without fight or argument will help to build that trust that is required for that "control freak" to ever be able to let go and develop confidence in themselves and others.

Every Dog has Its Day

One significant thing in our lives we have no hope to control is time. Humanity is very preoccupied with time. Whether it is our fear of death, our need to worry about something to feel important or needed, or a way to measure or judge our lives - we are focused on being on time, in time, timeouts, overtime, remember that time, time after time, in real time, time marches on, Father Time, time sheets, keep time, time machines...you get the picture. Actually, the fixation with time seems to be a relatively new phenomenon of modern, first world societies and most definitely is not a universal concern. This indifference to time you can find in other cultures is actually used against them to justify negative stereotypes and condemnations of those cultures as lazy and not hardworking. Even negative judgments are made of an individual in regards to time, if people do not show up to an appointment on time they are disorganized, lazy, or disrespectful. I am not saying that time does not have a usefulness or that time is unnecessary, but it seems to me that a fixation on time creates stress and negative judgements. As with all things, there should be a balance. A balance between not suffering panic or anxiety from concerns about time versus not procrastinating, not delaying living your life and thereby missing out on it. When living our lives - time has relevance but it can often be used against you by others or even yourself. If you feel that you are too late, you won't bother; if you are too soon, you will wait - both have the same result of inaction. For a culture so fixated on time, we likely waste more of it than any other, given the allowances of conveniences now found in our lives. We do not need to be spending every hour of every day on our survival and we live longer lives than ever before in human history. Perhaps we can afford to waste some time - maybe we can worry less about it, and use that energy instead to focus on each other - doing more with and for one another. Perhaps our survival does require us spending hours each day working towards ensuring it - working towards a sustainable existence, maybe it's worth it to sacrifice some of our modern conveniences to spend more time protecting and repairing our environment, our world, and those creatures in it. When running the kennel I wanted to focus on spending time with the dogs and

Sometimes you just have to stop to smell the daffodils

caring for those pets in our care and not spending all day sitting in an office - so we structured our schedule around the dogs and had all visits, check-ins, and check-outs done by appointment. In doing so, we could manage our time accordingly without sacrificing any time needed to care for the pets staying with us. The problem being often people were rather avant garde about their appointment times and would show up early or late without much regard to the amount of juggling and planning that goes into caring for a large number of pets. It was the most consistent frustration for me. I initially took it as disrespect for us and what we do. It would stress me out, especially if we needed to do walks around the appointments scheduled. Of course, I allowed for the reasonable. I know that things can happen, but when clients would be over 2 hours late without any sort of word by phone, text, or email, it would upset our schedule and my emotional state. There were even those that showed up an hour early to an off-hours early morning appointment (at a time that they had just set themselves the night before)! That caused stress and friction even in the relationship between the clients - who just expected to be served when they arrived the hour earlier and our team that had to cut other animal's care windows short to try to appease the unreasonable. However, I did come to realize that my stresses over the schedule were pointless, as all too often people being early or late often worked out to best accommodate events - even those completely unpredictable things that will naturally just happen when dealing with so many dogs, so many cats, and so many people and appointments. So while we always did have clients schedule appointment times, we let go of structuring the schedule completely around them. We often found that in just doing what needed to be done, when it needed to be done, the appointments would just naturally fall into place as they were supposed to – as nature or the universe or whatever you may believe, intended.

A great example of this is one weekend when we were having approved adopters coming to meet one Humane Society dog while we also had a few of the other Humane Society dogs out to an event. The dogs attending the event were supposed to be back well before our afternoon walks while the meet and greet between adopters and adoptable dog was supposed to occur at the time those walks. It was common to schedule these events concurrently so the potential adopters could walk the dog they were considering adopting while we had the others out. Planning in this way ensured all the dogs remained on the same schedule. However, the adopters got lost and the volunteers transporting the dogs home from the event were delayed. We walked all the dogs when required and the adopters show up right as we were finishing up. The adopters were familiar with our work with retired Sled dogs and had come to meet sweet Kusko, in hopes of rescuing one of these fearful but magical dogs. So we brought her out to meet them - but that did not last long. It was not a match as she was simply not interested in any connection with them and her fear level was through the roof. As I had someone take her back to the kennel, we discussed what they were looking for in a dog since their first choice was not a fit and none of the other Sled dogs were options for various reasons. They were disappointed but definitely understood and agreed Kusko was not the dog for them. I was just starting to consider other dogs in care when the volunteer pulled up with the dogs from the event. Ack! My immediate concern was what inconvenient timing! None of this group were of interest to the adopters - they wanted a medium sized dog and were hoping to connect with a retired Sled dog. This group pulling into the driveway included two older small dogs and an extra large dog, Fay, a Saint Bernard mix. Given my helper was still busy settling Kusko back in, I had to excuse myself from speaking with the family looking to adopt to receive the returning dogs and get them into a secure yard. As fate would have it, I took the two small dogs in first and had to leave Fay in our driveway with the volunteer and the adopters. By the time I came back out, the magic had already happened. This family and Fay were smitten with each other. The family that wanted a medium, Sled dog were suddenly aware of the strong but inexplicable connection between them and this Saint Bernard mix. For Fay, the big dog that was nervous of men and cars - was following the husband around the parking lot eagerly and without hesitation jumping happily into the back of their van when he sat down in it.

A happy Fay out on a walk one evening before she was adopted

Even their small dog, who could be timid of larger dogs, adored Fay and was relaxed and playful with her. It was just meant to be - so it was. That is how time works in truth. All things happen when they are meant to and it seems like trying to force time only causes stress, frustration, and hurt.

Dogs are not concerned with time. Dogs live in the moment. Dogs do not fret over the past and do not have anxiety about the future. Dogs are present - they learn behaviors and can develop or have fears from past experiences but they really seem to not hold the past against each other. They expect the best in any given situation and are willing to move on from transgressions within moments of any altercation or insult. Once the energy settles and levels out, they move on. Dogs do not procrastinate - if they want to do something, they surely are not waiting unless you make them. By not putting things off, dogs accomplish what they set out to do without concern about failure or it being too soon or too late. They will chase that toy, play with that dog, chew that bone or run along a beach all with joy and free of ego. If they never catch the toy, the other dog doesn't want to play, the bone gets taken away, or they have to get put on their leash at the beach - that does not affect the vigor they attempt to do the same again. Dogs will continue to try, and keep trying, with an unfailing joy and lightness of spirit that helps to buoy their efforts. Dogs are not concerned about being too old or too young - they just do, in the moment, what they see or feel needs to be done. They do not wait - they just do. This approach not only allows them to accomplish things efficiently - it is also healthier in that they are actively doing something, not overthinking it and not getting crippled by anxiety. If the dog tries and fails, even if the Frisbee gets lost in a tree or on a roof so they will never have that Frisbee again - that does not decrease their desire for play, for toys, or even for other Frisbees. Some would say dogs never learn when to quit, but that continued pursuit of what they want is key to their success. Dogs typically rely on human beings to provide for them - so they are lucky to not worry about pride or insecurities when it comes to reminding their humans to let them out, take them for a walk, feed them, or give them some love. Often when people have to keep reminding their loved ones of their needs, it will hurt our feelings and can cause us to feel unloved and doubt our worth. Dogs do not seem to be overly concerned about being forgotten about or dismissed at any one time, as they will continue to follow you around your house with a toy to toss, nuzzle your hand for more pets, and whine at the door to go out. Some dogs will even bring you their empty food bowl to let you know if you have forgotten to feed them! They do not take offense, they move forward with positive expectation of you doing what they want and need. Humanity would be well served to learn from this mentality about time that dogs seem to live in. Humans living in the moment would experience less stress since they are not worrying about past shortcomings and they are not wrapped up in anxiety about how something will or will not work out. They would be healthier just from the physicality of taking action in the moment and not overthinking or procrastinating. In addition, they would be happier for not dwelling on the past - for forgiving, for not taking offense, for letting go and moving on with life - in doing so, we could leave a lot of dysfunction behind. By moving forward and not continuing to revisit past failures of our friends, family and ourselves we can break free from the negative impacts of those failures and focus completely on new attempts to succeed. If we can also let go of our fixation on time and expectations or attempts to control it, we could embrace the natural timing of things. This would allow us to stress less, reduce our insecurities and take less offense - which all would contribute to a greater level of happiness and contentedness. If we could just go with the flow, or "Let go and let God" - we allow ourselves to fail, we accept it as simply life and we move forward and continue to try. Just think of those things in your life that you did not achieve simply because you did not try or did not continue to try after failing once or twice. How many success stories do we read or hear about that happened simply because the person refused to give up despite failure and rejection? What things could we still accomplish in our lives if we simply accepted that something could happen – but when it is supposed to happen not simply when we think it should? What sort of freedom does that allow us? How would it be if our families did not continuously mention our past mistakes? It is TIME to loosen our grip on our attempts to control time and stop trying to meet some sort of deadline that society or simply our expectations dictate. We need to live in the moment and not let our past negatively affect our future. This is where one can find success they never expected, happiness they did not think possible, and freedom they did not know existed. Paying attention to the present and not concerning ourselves too much with what is past or what is to come, is what we can do and appreciate.

Back in high school drama class, our wonderful teacher Mrs. Beaven ran us through a social exercise. We were to take turns assuming various positions in a scene on-stage. The instructions were simply to go on stage and assume a position or stance of power over the other individual on stage. There was to be no words - just all body language - on an empty stage, except for a couch. If your position was perceived as stronger of the two on stage, you remained - weaker then you took your leave of the stage. It started out with people sitting versus standing; standing was more powerful. Standing relaxed versus standing akimbo versus standing in aggressive posture, standing as an aggressor was strongest. A few people took turns, trying different stances, none took the power away. Then another student, Colleen, got up on stage and did something that surprised us all. In the face of the aggressive posture of the other student, she turned her back to him, sat down, and looked off into the distance, with zero acknowledgment on her face of his presence. That indifference won the day! By paying no attention to the other actor, that actor had no value to her, no power over her. It was a very significant lesson to learn in regards to humanity and human nature. Indifference is power, ignoring something robs it of any value.

When we "Like" and "Share" it does show some support and attention for our friends and family. However, despite our connected world we are truly more disconnected than ever. The more attention we pay to the screen, is less attention for those things in our lives that are really important. What are our actions and choices telling those in our lives about their worth to us? When we are ever engaged with those things on a screen and not with those with whom we live with, work with, and play with - what does that tell those others about their importance to us? By our choosing to pay our attention to a screen and not connecting with our loved ones - that damages our relationships. Those who seek out connections with us will be hurt, resentful, and frustrated which then affects our next efforts to connect with them later. We are all too checked out of our lives, where we are physically present but not truly there for anyone in our lives. And that is what dogs have also taught me - that giving your attention to something gives it value.

Sometimes even hidden toys were discovered!

If you are wanting to play with your dog you can pick up a stick that has been lying on the ground for weeks. It is just a stick. Nothing special really, and likely one of many on the ground - but you use that stick to play with your dog by selecting it, holding it, talking about it, waving it around, as you get your dog excited to fetch this new treasure. A sure way to have that stick have no special meaning after a few fetches is to pay attention to something else - to redirect your dog's attention to a new thing that now has value magically, and the stick is easily forgotten once it has none of your energy on it. Dogs in a pack are similar, each is paid attention to as they all socialize and exercise. They interact with each other, wrestle, sniff, follow along in a group maybe even chase. Introduce a toy item to the pack and you have a completely new dynamic to overcome. Dogs with toys love to play through tugging and fetching, if other dogs are around they will often vie for possession of the toy, perhaps even toss it about to get other dogs interested in order to have the others chase that dog in order to get the toy. It can be quite funny to watch as the dogs chase the toy and each other. They will often tease each other with the toy to engage more and more dogs in the play session. There was an apple orchard on the property where we did our pack walks and it was always very comical when the dogs would chase each other to possess the one stick or apple that another dog had chosen. A dog simply had to select one stick or apple and once that was the one that had the attention, that object was the prized possession with all the value. There were literally dozens upon dozens of apples and sticks around the property that were ignored, they were not picked up, so they had no value and none sought to have them. Unfortunately, instead of paying attention to any of the other hundred apples on the ground the dogs would even potentially get nasty and try to fight over the one. That is when we would have to step in with all our energy and attention focused on another apple that we would redirect the value to but we would maintain possession over.

That is why we could not have toys in our packs - it could

trigger fights. If a dog found or had a toy, their focus on it made it a high value item that other dogs took notice of and then wanted. Heaven help us if it squeaked or made a noise, that attracted the attention of a group of other dogs to that toy and then every dog in the pack wanted the toy. With so many dogs wanting the one toy, it could start aggression amongst the group for who would have possession over it. Some may say that simply having a great number of toys would remedy this but in our experience, whatever toy had the attention of one dog could quickly have the attention of the pack. Then that one toy had all the value and the other toys were forgotten and ignored (remember the bounty of apples and sticks?). It was a dreaded sound on walks - the squeaker of a toy! Then the concern to figure out who had a toy and how to get that toy away without alerting the whole pack to its existence. If you panicked and tried to catch the dog and the toy, it was suddenly a chaotic game of chase with the occasional aggressive overture amongst the dogs. So we learned that pursuing the dog with the toy was frivolous and had the effect of upsetting the pack in the exact way we were trying to avoid. So the tactic to avoid conflict, ignore the toy and the dog with it while showering our attention and energy onto other dogs and perhaps even other objects like sticks to offset and disrupt the toy attraction. Then once the toy was left behind, we could nonchalantly scoop it up and hide or dispose of it without a show.

The pack always got along best when just allowed to be themselves with themselves. Without toys, with just the focus, attention, and affection shared with each other. They would play with one another, groom one another, follow one another, snuggle one another - their interaction was always the best way to maintain well-balanced dog health and behavior. We can learn from this further, that focusing on the material in life and not on each other, we lose that socialization that is so critical to our overall health and behavior. Interacting with others not only provides you with a support network in your community, friends, and family, but also develops your social skills to get along with other people in a helpful and amicable way. Through having those people skills you will be more active, you will engage with others, give more of yourself towards the needs of others, and find those opportunities for self-actualization as part of the highest self we can attain in Maslow's Hierarchy. That is who we can grow to be. We can be a person whose value is immeasurable in the lives of those they know. You will build your value of self beyond measure, not defined or limited by dollar signs, clothes labels, or car you drive. Give of yourself, your time, your attention and make a genuine difference in your world and in yourself.

It is not just good enough to appreciate the now; you have to be present in it. You have to recognize and engage with those who are most important to you. In our ever-expansive society and given the worldwide reach of technology, more than ever friends and family are spread out across geographies that even just one generation ago was unheard of. Personally, I have good friends around the world, including literally on the opposite side of the globe, and my

Show and share love with those you care about

family lives throughout North America. It is easy to appease your guilt of being so far away through the use of social media, video chats, phone calls and texts to keep connected as best you can with those you hold dear in life. I know all too well that using technology to keep in touch can really just seem like a battle of distractions as you see your mother's eyes wander to the television or realize your father is playing solitaire on his computer while you are on FaceTime with them. I will do it to when trying to work or listen to something and I realize too late that I have no idea what my son has said to me - and he is standing only a few feet away! I realize there are many things going on in our lives and distractions are always present. The problem is that the distractions cause a very deliberate disconnect and that disconnect or distraction can hurt your loved one's feelings and thereby negatively affect your relationship. We know we need to see each other, we know that is the goal. We have all sorts of excuses for not getting together, too busy, other commitments, travel is expensive. Honestly though, nothing beats in-person interactions for truly connecting with each other. Simply looking at someone's profile page or chatting with them via video, phone, or text does not provide a true connection. We all know this but it is dogs that prove it. Most pet owners have attempted to connect with their dogs when they are out of town by calling out to them over the phone or video chat with little to no success. It is not the same as talking to people of course but that in itself demonstrates that there is indeed a significant element missing in these interactions. We need to make more time for people, especially those we have or want a real connection with. Think about how often you misinterpret the tone or the intent of a text, an email, or social media post. That real connection, that real relationship building comes from making the time and the effort to do so. Strong interpersonal connections are made in person, from sharing space with one another, making eye contact, providing hugs and pats on the back. In person, tone and intent become more obvious and your support and caring are easily provided. You can share those moments that are not edited, are not scripted, are not cropped nor filtered - you share reality with someone. In that reality is where we find the truth in our relationships and build those connections with others that have a strength, a permanence, and a trust. Those relationships that mean most to us all have that direct connection in common. We are losing our way when we focus too much on how many "Friends", "Followers" and "Subscribers" we have, rather than on the truth of who we are and who we have in our lives that we love and rely on. We lose a certain depth or substance - are we weakening our characters? Are we sacrificing depth to achieve breadth? Is it that we are spread so thin that we cannot afford to give much of ourselves anymore? It does take an investment of yourself - your time, your energy, your money to make those in-person meetings happen. We are supposed to live in a world of convenience and have so much spare time but it does seem that we struggle more than ever for that time and to have the energy to invest in getting together or making connections with people. Often those in-person interactions require effort that people just do not want to offer because they are so drained from the day-to-day strains of their lives. We devote so much time to social media, to our phones, to our jobs, to our television programs, to commuting; we do not have much left. Add in the increased time spent doing for our children, and more time and effort devoted to pet ownership, the less time we have for one another.

I look at my grandmother - she was the one person in my life who I never questioned her love for me. It was not because she always told me - in fact, it was only quite late in her life that I made a point of telling her that I loved her and she told me I was silly as she returned the sentiment with a blushing smile. The woman was fierce before that word was used in that context. She was devoted to her family, to her friends, and to her community like no other I have known. She did work but not when I knew her - so I am sure it could be argued that she had more time because of retirement. However, it was who she was, not acquired behavior late in life. When I think of Grandma's life and the relationships she had, those were born of her involvement - her activity and active participation in the lives of those she shared love and community with. There was no one that was more giving of herself to any person in need. Her family, her neighbors, her friends, strangers - if you needed help, Gwen would readily give it. Regardless of who you were, where you were from, what religion you were, or how you were dressed - she cared. She was genuine and authentic. She cared for you but she would definitely let you know if she felt you were making wrong choices. She shared and valued her morals and belief in treating others with consideration and respect. She may not always agree with another person but she would always, without pause, be there for him or her however they needed. Grandma was connected to her family, her friends, and her community in real and meaningful ways. That is how people once were. Family lived closer, we knew our neighbors, we were involved in the community - we were more engaged in our reality.

We used to seek out real connections with each other. Dogs continue to seek out connections - they make the effort to connect with each other and with you. They do not only want to bark or howl to connect from afar - they want to see each other, smell each other, lick each other, run up on each other: play, wrestle, chase, or even just relax in the vicinity of one another. I found that I could not be on the phone - a call, messaging, or even just checking Facebook - while I was leading a pack walk. The dogs just knew immediately if you were there physically but not mentally. They could sense the disconnect and would alter their behavior accordingly. I would lose the connection to the dogs if I "checked out" by being on my phone. That was an obvious lesson for me and a rule I always had to follow for the welfare of the pack. Checking out on my phone, had negative repercussions for the relationship I should be connected with. With our attention on technology, we are not present. Our energy, our focus, our priority is focused elsewhere. Sometimes we need a break, yes. Nevertheless, it is out of control how often we are zombified by our screens. One loses touch with reality and your own sense of self. You get lazy, squander opportunities, you achieve nothing – the biggest effort you will muster in a day or about a cause is clicking "Like." If you are really passionate about a cause "Share." Heck, you might go crazy and even sign an online petition! We seek connection, however even our closest humans are all too often disconnected from us and the environment. I hate going out to supper with my family and we are all on our phones rather than talking to one another. All too often nowadays we are devoting too much of our time and attention to the things that do not truly matter much in our lives. How often are you trying to engage with someone only to discover when you glance over that they are not listening to you because they are playing a game on their smartphone, scrolling through social media on their tablet, or watching the television? If your family is anything like the typical home, then this has occurred to you. I know it happens to me frequently. Yes, I have heard the justifications for it - just wanting to level up in a game, keeping in touch with family and friends from afar, or even the simple request to wait until a commercial break to have the conversation or answer the question. Despite us sharing a home, a meal, or even a room - we are no longer sharing ourselves with one another. At least not in an authentic and true way. Some would argue that we share more of ourselves than ever with our social media profiles. However, it is rare that our social media posts are true windows into our lives. We can choose which angle for the perfect profile picture, use a filter, crop out the embarrassing objects in the background and use these facades to tell the world that is who we are. Just that one moment, those limited number of characters, that meme or viral video - that is what we share of ourselves with the world. We tend to only project the best of ourselves - we go with the theory that perception is reality. So, although we share more information than ever before for the world to see - depending on our privacy settings, we are not actually sharing our true selves in meaningful ways.

There is not a plethora of stories about dogs not connecting genuinely because they seek that out. However, one lesson about dogs and their connections can be learned from observing dogs "fence fighting." Fence fighting is when dogs essentially patrol a fence or physical divide of some sort. Almost always putting a fence between two dogs will make them bark at one another. Sometimes it can even look very aggressive and dangerous. Fence fighting only requires some physical divide that creates a level of disconnect and

Open that gate and make a connection – remove barriers in order to connect

removal of accountability, from the other dog. Most of our walks with the packs of the dogs were simply a circuit tour around the property. We would go from the far back northwest corner up to the southeast and back again. Exploring our way through the different yards, orchard, tree lines, and bushes. These circuits were done off leash and the dogs would all go at their own pace with the freedom to get distracted by play or exploring some smells they discover. This freedom helped the dogs to feel relaxed and confident and to get the level of exercise and socialization suitable for them. What could happen though, with such freedom allowed, is that the group of dogs that were walking with me would essentially lap other dogs. Our pack would be spread out through the property and we would end up meeting up with each other at the gate of one of the large yards. This yard occupied a large corner of the front of the property so as we headed back from the front gate, we would include it as part of our route. As I would approach the back of the yard, the dogs still in the orchard would rush up to the fence to greet me and the other dogs coming towards them. The dogs walking with me would also rush up to the fence and gate of the yard in anticipation of our route and to meet the dogs rushing up from the other side. Despite the dogs all knowing each other, walking together, and getting along - since there was a fence in between them - fence fighting would inevitably occur. Up and down the fence line the dogs would run, chasing and barking and snarling at one another. Quite the production to be sure. I specifically use "production" in this context because all it took was for me to open the gate and I would joke about which dog won the Oscar for that show. Simply opening the gate and removing the divide, the dogs were once again connected and accountable to one another and all was harmonious once again.

Much like our interactions on social media - we are indeed disconnected from reality and our true selves and accountability on our social media profiles. This disconnect from reality on social media platforms makes us tend to easily "bark" at one another in various comments, tweets, and posts that are typically bolder and perhaps more vicious than we would ever be in person. This type of behavior further proves that true connection allows for healthier relationships in all sorts of ways. We are not accomplishing anything real – we are not out connecting with others, connecting with nature, connecting with truth – then wonder why we struggle for esteem, happiness, health, and relationships. The truth we so often forget or deny is that our "outside" - our looks, our actions, our choices - are merely a projection of what is "inside." If we spend all our time only sharing facades we degrade the value of our true selves. Dogs are not worried about facades and what others think of their looks and behavior - if you think they do, you have not had your dog lick his private parts in the middle of your living room when your new boss is over for supper. Dogs concern themselves with living - they are not insecure about being too fat, too skinny, too tall, and too messy - heck, our motto was often "a muddy dog is a happy dog!" Dogs are consistently seeking connection - they seek out our love, a pet, a nuzzle, even just sitting on our foot or leaning on our leg. It does not matter how, the dogs just want a connection, a real connection. Dogs are content when they are connected with those with whom they share a bond. It is best for their emotional and physical health to have those interactions that are in person and that is what is best for us too. Dogs realize that they actually feel better, more energized, more confident and happier, when they have those real connections with one another. We need to know that we benefit from those real connections too. Sharing space and experiences with one another allows you to have a genuine connection. You benefit through knowing they love and care for you as you - not just a profile picture. Our screens give us plenty of headaches and heartaches, let's not be so hesitant to walk away from them to engage in truly connecting with our friends and families. Social media should just complement those true relationships in our lives, enhancements of our understanding of one another and the opportunity to keep up with one another in those times that we are unable to get together in person. Electronic devices should not replace real life, real people, and real experiences. Devices that are praised for allowing us to stay "connected" actually seem to do the exact opposite. We are losing our connections with one another. We need to take the initiative to check back in to our lives and those in them.

We need to appreciate all that we already have - to genuinely feel and express gratitude. We need to pay attention to those things that already enrich our lives in any number of ways and not ignore what we may be blessed to have in our lives consistently. I remember being in grade ten and a group of friends were sitting around chatting. A couple of us had birthdays coming up soon which meant that we were about to be able to get our drivers licenses. One of our older friends just rolled his eyes at us and literally said "What's the big deal?" Well, it is easy enough for someone who has their license and drives every day to take that for granted. But for those that do have that privilege, it is a big deal because of the positive impacts it will have on their lives. Having a license of course allowed one greater independence and freedom, truly a coming of age moment in the lives of most young people. Of course there are many types of these examples, the desire (or expectation) to get married, the excitement of being engaged, and then in a sadly short length of time, taking one's spouse and the relationship for granted. One gets excited for a new job and within weeks is expressly dissatisfied, annoyed, or bored with the opportunity. We have a tendency to lack gratitude for the blessings and achievements in our lives. Dogs do not fall victim to this tendency though. They do not lose the magic; they retain that excitement and appreciation of almost every aspect of their lives. Dogs do this naturally, it is not something that is taught - in fact, we humans often try to teach them to let go of their gregarious appreciation in many circumstances. You can leave home for five days, five hours, or even just five minutes and your dog will be over the moon to have you return beyond all reason and logic (but it definitely makes you feel loved, appreciated, and important). Dogs get excited to eat, even if they do multiple times in a day. They get excited to go outside, even if they were just out a few minutes before. Dogs get excited to go with you in the car (if they aren't afraid of it!), even if last time you took them to the vet. The lesson here is obvious and undeniable - I do not need to share any story because we have all witnessed this behavior in dogs. We should readily accept that showing gratitude for those that we have chosen to treat as mundane or expected brings magic back into our lives. Your attention paid to people and things you have taken for granted will revitalize and enrich your relationship with them. Without costing you anything other than a change in your perspective, you can improve your life immeasurably.

Of course, it serves to reason that if paying attention to something gives it value then the reverse is true - ignoring something devalues it. If you notice one dog acting out of sorts or misbehaving - often the pack with turn away from that dog at that time. Even in dog training, they use that tactic in reaction to undesired behavior. If the dog barks, turn away; if the dog jumps up, turn away. Remember, if you pay attention to something it gains value, which is a reward. So if we continue to simply focus on our phones, computers, and televisions instead of our families, our work, our friends, even our health we are prioritizing those screens over those things that should be priority above anything else. No one lays on their deathbed wishing they had spent more time on Facebook, that they would have posted one more picture or shared one more meme. No one even lays on their bed at night and regrets not spending enough time in front of a screen. Screens remove you from the reality you are in. That disconnection provides us an escape, which sometimes you may need. However, as with all things, it should be all in balance, and our lives will only improve if we connect more with that which is truly important. It may require more effort than swiping a screen, but it is most definitely worth it. To love and be loved is ever important for our esteems and for our relationships with those that we share our hearts and homes with. Let's checkout less and check in more with those we love and make sure that we are giving them what they need from us. Let's be there for them and let's start to expect them to be there for us. Pay attention in life - pay attention to who you are, the choices you are making, and what is occurring around you - your life is important, you are important, and those people in your life that are important to you deserve at the very least your undivided attention on them and their lives. Connection is therapeutic. Connection gives us a support network that builds and maintains confidence and esteem to tackle life's challenges and overcome them in real ways. To be there for people in an authentic way, and not just to "Like" their post or "Retweet" their 140 (make that 280) characters or less. Seek out your people, seek out to connect with them - that is a great way to avoid regrets. Pay attention to what is truly important rather than the things that are not worthy of any.

Our attention in times of disaster, mistakes, and misfortune seems unhealthily fixed on blame. Our society is fixated on finding fault and placing blame - at the same time that we are less engaged and less accountable. We are less community focused and less likely to know our neighbors. We use social media to keep tabs rather than keep in touch. Those who do have causes that they champion seem to limit their involvement to armchair activism and rarely take any action outside of a mouse click and strokes on a keyboard. People avoid responsibility and getting involved. Everyone is staring at a screen seemingly unaware that life is happening all around them. Things you pay attention to are the things that have value. By devoting so much attention to our screens, we are demonstrating a lack of caring about those people, things, and places that we should be holding in the highest regard. What is happening is that we are not taking care of what we should be - we are lackadaisical in our lives but then complain when it does not go how we expect it to. I will not even talk politics but that is one example that jumps to mind immediately. On a more individual level - we do nothing to change our lifestyle but complain about being underweight or overweight; we do nothing to change our relationship but complain about being ignored, abused, or left; we do nothing to change our jobs but complain about our bosses, the customers, and not being paid enough. What I have observed is that if you do not take care of it (whatever that "it" may be), someone else will. I saw this numerous times in working with client's dogs and dogs surrendered by their owners. The complaint about the dog - "aggressive" behavior. It is simply heartbreaking how often a dog is blamed for behavior that occurs simply as a result of human action or inaction. So many dogs we worked with that I had been told were "aggressive" were actually not. I simply cannot bear to think of the hundreds, if not thousands, of dogs that have lost their lives in situations like that. Situations where a failure on the part of the humans, who are to provide for these dogs, creates canine behavior that results in the dog having to be euthanized. Here is the issue I saw repeated again and again, dogs would sometimes act "aggressive" - lunge, bark, growl - so therefore they were labelled aggressive. They were going to bite or kill something! Right?!?! Wrong. Once I would delve into the scenario details in which the problem behavior occurred it was ALWAYS in times when the security of the home, the human(s), or the dog was threatened AND the humans did nothing to provide protection from that threat. The human did not take care of the situation, thereby basically forcing the dog to take some sort of action. The human is then upset by the action the dog took and only blames the dog. If you are going to take issue with how your dog reacts in a situation, first question yourself and what guidance you have provided to the dog for them to know how and when to act and in what way. If you do not want your dog to protect you, then do not be weak. If you take care of yourself, your home and your dog - the dog will not feel the need to protect you. Your dog can relax and follow your lead. Yes, the unexpected can occur - that is when you have to have your dog's trust in you to take care of the situation. They know you are going to take care of whatever it is so they do not need to.

I remember we had a rescue come in from up north, Nomi. Nomi was intact and just finishing her heat. She was initially relaxed and respectful with the pack and played and socialized without issue. However, after a few days, something shifted in her energy that I noticed as we were just winding down a walk session. Nothing had happened but I swore something was different. Therefore, for the next round of walks, we started with just our two dogs that did not typically trigger other dogs. Bumble, our goofy and fun,

*Nomi happy
and relaxed
after her spay
(left)*

*Suni and I out
for some
exercise in the
orchard
(below)*

young male Husky and Great Pyrenees cross and Suni. Suni

was a wonderfully, happy and loving Black Lab cross -

always a big girl at over one hundred and twenty pounds but

she was never one to throw her weight around. She was

always more submissive and very respectful of other dogs.

My biggest concern was that Nomi was going to take issue or attack other females just because of her being intact and recently in heat. I was not worried about Suni though because in her long history (she was 12 years old at this time) with other dogs, she simply never upset another dog ever. Even proven dog-reactive dogs would not react to her. So with just Bumble and Suni out in the orchard, I went and retrieved Nomi. We came out and started our walk, Nomi approached Suni and without even sniffing or any attempt at introduction, she tried to attack her! She was trying to jump on Suni, latch on to her somehow, to engage her in a fight. Suni's response? She just looked at me in that moment with the look of "Are you going to take care of this or am I going to have to?" She did not react. This happened right in front of me so it was only a matter of a second, maybe two, before Nomi was separated from Suni. I took care of Suni, the threat she encountered, and we continued the walk with Nomi on leash. Suni was not at all injured and was completely unfazed by what happened. Nomi did not walk with the pack again until after she was spayed and recovered from the surgery. She never had another incident with any of the dogs in the pack - male or female. Once she returned to the pack she was right back to that original temperament of fun and respectful, even with Suni. Nomi's attack on Suni could have gone completely different. It could have been an extremely dangerous altercation that could have resulted in veterinary care being needed, long-term socialization issues for one or both of the dogs, or worst case - a dog being euthanized for hurting or killing another. None of that happened though because I took care of it. I stepped in, took responsibility for the interaction, and controlled it as best I could. It all turned out fine, not even a blip on either dogs' radar. It really was a non-issue but it is so memorable to me because of the look Suni gave me. My memory of that look still makes me smile because it was so surreal. Any other dog I can think of would have reacted but Suni knew I would not let her get hurt, she knew I would protect her and she looked to me to do so. It was a moment that really drove home the truth of the consequence of inaction. That it really is your own fault if you fail to do anything about a situation and then end up upset with the result. One cannot be upset that their dog is protective when they have that precise expectation of them! Living creatures are driven to survive. For dogs that involves ensuring that they, their pack, and their territory is not threatened. They will protect those things if they feel they are not secure or being protected. The "aggression" issue was the most serious but the all too common surrender of dogs that were 9-18 months old because they were full size dogs still behaving like puppies. Their behavior had not changed from their cute, little puppy days because their owners had neglected to train the dog, or worse, had reinforced the problem behaviors for a long time before taking issue with them. Dogs need to be taught how to live in our worlds, they need to know the rules and expectations of them while living with us in our homes. It is our responsibility as pet parents/owners to do this - even older dogs that are new to you, need to learn how to live with you.

You would not expect someone from another culture and who spoke another language to just know without guidance or assistance what our social norms are and how we run our households. Yet we expect dogs to. It is a grossly unreasonable expectation and our avoidance of responsibility is a real marker of weakness in who we are and what we are capable of. Blaming and judging others when we are too lazy or apathetic to do anything about that which we complain shows a need for greater depth of character and consistent adherence to a moral code. Rather than blame and judge others - choose to take action in your life, take responsibility for that which you can affect change, and take accountability when you know you should. Make a difference, make an effort, make good choices, and you will see your life and happiness improve as a result.

Time should be appreciated but it should not be rushed. It will not be rushed. It is best to not make decisions in a moment of panic. When we feel pressured by time, stressed, or in pain - this creates a panic state in which we struggle for rational thought. Stress does all sorts of bad things to our bodies and our brains. Excess stress can lead to weight gain, osteoporosis, digestive problems, hormone imbalances, cancer, heart disease, and/or diabetes - but it also affects cognitive functions. When we are panicked, we are not thinking clearly and not seeing beyond the immediate danger or stressor. We are making decisions - that are forced basically because of the stress creating an immediacy - but further compounded by the negative effects of that stress on our brain activity. When we are in a panic, we are choosing actions and reactions that are not typical and likely regretted. I learned this painful lesson from Wendell. Wendell was rescued from his life on a chain. A chain he had been put on as a puppy and that ended up embedding into his neck as he grew since he was neglected and never properly cared for. The chain - with a weight of nine pounds! - had to be surgically removed from his neck! What a horror story to have to live through. Wendell needed a break in life and found joy and love with us for his first few months in the

Wendell after his surgery, looking scary but feeling radically better (right)

The chain that Wendell was attached too when rescued (below)

Humane Society's care. He was initially nervous of the other

dogs - having lived outside on a chain creates such issues as

these dogs are often attacked by humans and dogs without

any means of escape. Wendell went for walks with just one

or two other dogs. Those dogs had to be very calm and not

overly interactive so that they would worry him at all. In the large yard, which the small group ran in, there was a large gate through which we could drive vehicles when necessary. Due to the size of the gate and the resulting gap between the two gate doors, there had been a "filler" piece of post bolted to one side of the gate so that no dogs could squeeze through the over-sized gap. It was a great thing to have to ensure the security of the yard - both coming and going. However, the fencer had installed the filler post in such a way - with two bolts about eight inches from both top and bottom - that there was a deep, narrow space between the post and the gate frame to which it was attached. On one particular day, I had just walked past the gate on the opposite side of where Wendell was, when I suddenly heard a dog screaming! I whirled around to see that Wendell was screaming in pain as his right front paw was somehow stuck in between the filler post and the gate frame. He must have jumped up on the gate and just happened to come down on the filler post thereby wedging his leg in the gap. He could not simply pull it out since his foot was wider than the part of the leg that was sitting wedged. He was stuck, he was in pain, and he was scared. I ran around to the far gate to get into the yard with him. I called the other two dogs out to the transition area in order to not cause any additional stressors for Wendell in this situation. I tried to settle Wendell down as much as possible with calm reassuring words, tone, and a gentle but deliberate touch near his hips. I wanted him to know I was there with him and there to help. I could not delay at all though since I knew he must be in pain in addition to reacting to being stuck - being tethered again! Poor Wendell! I told him it was okay and that I was going to get him out over his screams. I had to lift his leg to remove it from the wedge, which meant I had to get in a vulnerable position with a dog in a very volatile state. It had to be done – with no time to waste. I reached and connected with his elbow to raise him off and out. He reacted with an immediate lash of his head and he grabbed hold on my thigh and clamped down. Yes, he bit me. I did not let go of his leg, I stayed calm and as quick as he bit me, I had released his leg from the gate and we both let go. We both looked at each other with a bit of shock and relief. We were both happy that Wendell was free of his trap of sorts but he was shocked that he had bitten me. He actually seemed ashamed or embarrassed - perhaps even worried that I was going to punish him. He would not make eye contact and cowered around the yard. I reassured him that he did nothing wrong and that all I had for him was affection. Wendell had simply reacted to the pain and the stress, he was in a complete panic - of course, he would most likely have an atypical, even violent, reaction. As much as we were both shocked, I was well aware of the state he was in when I went to help him. I know his decision to bite was not really his choice but rather it was his panic that bit me, his "fight or flight" instinct. An instinct that had already been keenly sharpened to "fight" given his chain removing the "flight" option in his previous experiences. Wendell was a victim of his panic just as much as I was - and we both regretted his decision made in that state. In life, take the time necessary to make those important decisions. Try to recognize those times of panic or stress are not times to be making any decisions that are the best for you. You will be rushing into something that you will regret.

Regrets and mistakes can come back to haunt us all too often. Dysfunction in our relationships can come from errors and faults from the past never being forgotten and consistently being thrown back out again and again through the years. Sometimes through anger and other times through supposed humor but after years and years of one's mistakes being never forgotten it negatively impacts that person's esteem and the relationship that will never let them move on. Dogs do not have this same fixation with remembering and using the past against us. Dogs live very much in the moment and do not hang on to the past and previous errors in judgment and behavior. Dogs are not dysfunctional like that. If dogs did, I never would have been able facilitate any sort of rehabilitation for those dogs that needed it. Remember Cobb? If Rubius, Mamoa, and Minerva held on to past mistakes and missteps, they could never have helped Cobb to trust and engage other dogs. Each of the three were dogs that Cobb had tried to create an issue with when he first came into care. Rubius was a very tall, wolfhound mix that seemed to intimidate Cobb simply because of his size. He never did anything that should have upset or triggered Cobb but still Cobb would react aggressively if they were ever too close to one another. Mamoa was a Lab cross of some sort who had lost a leg to a cougar attack. Again, I did not ever witness Mamoa do anything that should have triggered Cobb. All I could guess was his gait was somewhat erratic because of the missing limb, that erratic movement could have confused and unnerved Cobb. Minerva, too, never did anything to trigger Cobb other than perhaps get too close for his comfort. They both liked to follow me out on walks so occasionally quarters could get too close behind me, regardless of the expanse of my behind! Each of these dogs had been a target of Cobbs aggression. None of them had done anything to justify Cobbs reaction to them. They had not initiated any issue, rather they had done nothing but simply exist in Cobb's vicinity. Any offense, space violation, or instigation was Cobbs and Cobbs alone. However, when Cobb was introduced to the pack again when I felt he was ready to do so, he was not confronted by any that he had irrationally targeted. None came for payback and none avoided or ignored him. He was welcomed back into the pack. The

An all-new Cobb, feeling happy and healthy back with the pack

other dogs engaged him in playing, exploring, and socializing. They had moved on because Cobb had. Cobb had changed. He had gotten better. Cobb was no longer that reactionary mess of a dog who was in pain and thought the other dogs were out to get him. If all the pack focused on were first impressions, so many dogs would have never had the opportunity to rehabilitate. They would never have found forever families to share their home and heart with. Dogs do not hold another's past against them. They see them as they are in the moment and seem to use shared history to build trust. Even if one makes a mistake or hurts them, they do not seem to be impeded from still sharing a connection with one another. It is inspiring. It is another aspect of how they love unconditionally. It is yet another reason to recognize that we can learn valuable lessons from our best friends.

BFFs:
Best FUR-iends FUR-ever

What a novel idea. Imagine humans learning from dogs! Such a seemingly odd notion but so intuitively right and, in my opinion, long overdue. Dogs are known as "man's best friend" so who better to provide insights and lessons to us. Who would we trust, respect, and love enough to listen to without our own insecurities and issues getting in the way? Painful lessons are best to come from a best friend.

Humanity needs to shift off this path of ego, greed, and hatred that only seems to have us hurtling toward some sort of destructive end. We have somehow lost our way. We need a new path to follow. Dogs have long been our companions and for centuries have walked with us, so why not let them show us a new way or simply the way back to where we should be?

From my observations and experiences, dog and humans seem to share not only history but also basic needs of survival and existence along with social dynamics. We both need water, food, shelter, security along with love and connections to thrive. Our similarities make the love and connection between our species easy but it is through our differences that we can learn the greatest lessons. Dogs are different from humankind in some critical ways that would only serve to improve our lives and the lives of those around us.

Just loving life, in the moment, with no fear of judgement

Dogs love unconditionally and openly, do not judge others, and are quick to see truth.

Dogs have an authenticity, without any hint of cynicism.

Dogs have an innocence, without naivety.

Dogs trust and accept without being gullible.

Dogs just free to be dogs, to play, to love, to live

I understand humans believe themselves to be the superior species but given our shared history with dogs, it only makes sense that our "best friend" could have some lessons for us to learn from.

Dogs have taught me so many valuable lessons, they have been a gift to me in my life - even, very literally, saving it - *thanks Snuffy!* Lessons on how to love more openly and honestly. Dogs modeled tolerance and accepting others for who they are. They paid attention to those they shared their lives with and sought genuine connections with them. Dogs have honoured truth even if it was awkward, painful, or challenging in the moment. While they do get affected by pain, much like we do, dogs strive to overcome pain – they do not wallow in it. Dogs are accountable to others and take responsibility for themselves. They live in the moment and never let go of the excitement for those things in their life that they enjoy. Dogs are magic in those ways. That magic can defy logic and reason but it most certainly exists. That magic that dogs bring to our lives touches our hearts and connects with our souls. The magic that fills you up beyond capacity the more you start to share it yourself. The magical gift of giving to others, rather than always taking, manages to not deplete you but rather keeps you fulfilled. Just look at dogs - with respect and appreciation - and you will see what they are trying to teach you and know the truths of those lessons in your head, heart, and gut. Then when you come to a crossroads and want to choose the right path, all you need to do is ask yourself "What would dogs do?"

What would we do?

Made in the USA
San Bernardino, CA
19 December 2018